CW00499491

GCSE Business

for Edexcel

Paul Hoang, Margaret Ducie and **Sam Cleary**

informe

ISBN 978-1-78014-055-1

Anforme Ltd, Stocksfield Hall, Stocksfield, Northumberland NE43 7TN.
Typeset by George Wishart & Associates, Whitley Bay.
Printed by Potts Print (UK) Ltd.

Contents

Chapter 1.1.1

The dynamic nature of business

Aims

By the end of this chapter, students should be able to understand:

- why new business ideas come about: changes in technology, changes in what consumers want, and products and services becoming obsolete.
- how new business ideas come about: original ideas, and adapting existing products/services/ideas.

Why new business ideas come about

Businesses exist to produce goods and services to satisfy the needs and wants of individuals, for which they hope to earn a profit and fulfil other objectives such as: increasing market share, survival, being the market leader or being a socially responsible business (see Chapter 1.3.1). Businesses produce new goods and services for many reasons including, changes in technology, new tastes and preferences and goods and services becoming obsolete. To stay competitive businesses may also introduce new products or services or adapt existing goods and services to fill gaps in the market.

Changes in technology

Technology is constantly evolving and new products and services are created as a result. Businesses such as Apple introduce new products to the market such as the Apple Watch. The Apple Watch is product-oriented as Apple designed and made a product which it hoped is attractive to consumers (rather than producing a watch that was based on market research conducted by the firm). Innovative and high-tech products are often product-oriented.

The growth of the internet has changed the way in which we communicate, store and access information. There has been an increase in the demand for mobile apps for smartphones and laptops. Businesses such as Facebook, Twitter, Instagram and Snapchat provide social media platforms. Almost all businesses have websites and this has created a need for web designers and computer programmers.

The increased use of smartphones has also led to greater demand for earphones, headphones and other accessories (such as cases, screen protectors, cleaning liquids and chargers). Cloud computing services are necessary for storing files, photographs and other information. Businesses such as Dropbox and Box have created storage and sharing facilities. The market for such services continues to grow and evolve.

Businesses such as Microsoft, Apple and Adobe continue to create and update software to use with their hardware.

The growth in digital radio, digital television, e-books, digital films and digital photographs has created new openings for software designers, sharing platforms, website designers and sites where people can publish their work. There are openings for shared workspaces offering Wi-Fi, meeting spaces and refreshment facilities.

Changes in what people want

People's needs change over time and businesses exist to meet these needs. For example, in the UK there has been an increase in demand for foods for people with specialist diets, such as gluten-free food and non-dairy milk drinks and therefore businesses start to provide them. People need external battery packs for smartphones, plugs with USB connections and businesses produce new products and adapt existing products to meet these needs.

Giving experiences such as a hot air balloon ride to people as a gift is a growing trend.

The increase in online shopping has increased the demand for delivery services. This includes greater demand for food deliveries to offices, schools and homes.

Giving experiences to people as a gift is also a growing trend. The increased use of social media has contributed to this trend as people like to post pictures and videos of themselves, doing interesting things, on platforms such as Instagram and Facebook. This has created a demand for such experiences, for example bread baking, pottery, martial arts lessons, attending football matches, driving a classic car, a hot air balloon ride, swimming with dolphins, action holidays and volunteer experiences.

Products and services becoming obsolete

Some products and services have become obsolete such as non-digital cameras, CDs and DVDs. This means that businesses such as photograph developers and retailers that sell CDs and DVDs face minimal demand for their products, so will eventually go out of business. Apple's iPhone, first launched in June 2007, introduced the world to the use of smartphones on a mass scale, making analogue and digital phones obsolete products.

How new business ideas come about: original ideas

Original products are created such as driverless cars and drones. Airbnb and Uber are examples of a new business model which is completely digital and relies on the concept of a sharing economy. Airbnb and Uber allow flexibility for employees as well as customers. As soon as one firm enters a market and is successful other firms will enter the market in an attempt to take some of the available profits.

Businesses are created to fill gaps in the market or because a person has an original idea. In 2007, Shaun Pulfrey, a hair stylist from London, had an idea for a hairbrush designed to detangle hair easily. He created the Tangle Teaser hairbrush, which is now available in many designs, sizes and shapes and his business empire is worth £200 million.

Adapting existing products/services/ideas

Extension strategies are used to prolong the life of products. Nestle produces KitKats in different flavours, for example: orange, green tea, cookies and cream. It produces limited editions and bars in different sizes.

Toothbrush and toothpaste manufacturers frequently create new features and qualities in their toothbrushes, for example, bristles which fade to indicate when a new brush should be purchased and toothpaste for people with sensitive teeth. Soft drink manufacturers adapt drinks to have zero calories and natural sweeteners instead of artificial, e.g. Coca-Cola Life is sweetened with stevia, a natural sweetener. Lego revitalised the brand by creating Lego models based on films and books such as Star Wars and The Hobbit and creating Lego 'Friends' which is aimed at girls.

Old and existing products and services sometimes become fashionable again such as Silver Cross prams, scooters for children and traditional barbers that provide grooming services to cater for the current fashion of men with beards.

Exam style question

Identify the reasons why the following businesses came about:

(a) Furniture shop specialising in vintage furniture.

(b) A bed and breakfast offering an authentic 1940s experience.

(c) An online business where you can send a 'cream tea' (scones, cream, jam and tea) as a gift.

(d) A cloud based storage facility for photographs and personal files.

(e) An app enabling the user to find the best mode of transport in their location.

(f) A producer of gluten free snacks. *(6 marks)*

Chapter review questions

1. State three reasons why new business ideas come about.
2. Give an example of how technology has created a new business idea.
3. Give an example of a good or service which has become obsolete.
4. State two ways new business ideas come about.
5. Explain why a business may adapt an existing product.

Key terms

Goods are physical items which are produced by businesses, e.g. cars, lipstick, toys, cups and saucers.

Market orientation occurs when a business designs and makes a product which takes into account the needs and wants of consumers.

Needs are essential goods and services necessary for survival.

Product orientation occurs when a business designs and makes a product which it hopes will be attractive to consumers.

Services are non-physical items such as a haircut, a guitar lesson, and a manicure.

Wants are goods and services which are desired by individuals and firms.

Chapter 1.1.2

Risk and reward

Aims

By the end of this chapter, students should be able to understand:

- the impact of risk on business activity: business failure, financial loss, and lack of security.
- the impact of reward on business activity: business success, profit, and independence.

Risk and reward

There are many factors which influence whether or not businesses are successful and it is necessary for people who start businesses to accept the risk of failure for the chance of success and rewards.

Risk: Business failure

A decision to set up a business has an element of risk as there is always a chance that the business may fail. Even with meticulous planning and market research, a business may provide goods or services that few people wish to buy.

The business may have chosen to produce or sell products that are no longer in high demand, such as mobile phones, CDs, and DVDs. An upmarket restaurant or shop selling expensive gifts may have been opened during a downturn in the economy (see Chapter 1.5.4) and because both are considered to be luxuries for most people they may be unsuccessful.

The location of a business may be unknown to people or difficult to get to, and therefore the business may not thrive.

Competition in the market may be high and therefore a business may not attract enough customers to remain in business. For example, a shop selling clothing in a small town may not attract enough customers to remain in business. It may be difficult for an independent café to attract enough customers to compete with multinational chains of coffee shops such as Starbucks, Pret a Manger, Café Nero and Costa Coffee.

Risk: Financial loss

All businesses require start-up capital and working capital (healthy cash flow) for day-to-day expenses. They aim to make a profit by covering costs with income from sales. There are many reasons why a business may face the risk of financial loss, such as when it becomes difficult to collect money owed to them from customers.

Other reasons why there is a risk of financial loss include:

- Interest rates (see Chapter 1.5.4) going up, which makes loan repayments more expensive.
- Lack of customers causing monthly income to be less than outgoings.
- A recession or downturn in the economy (see Chapter 1.5.5), causing customers to spend less on goods and services.
- A major emergency such as a flood, fire, or burglary.
- A health and safety crisis, for example, a restaurant causing customers to get food poisoning.

Risk: Lack of security

Entrepreneurs take a risk because they are employed by their own business and may suffer from a lack of security in the form of regular income, especially in the initial stages of the business startup. If they are a sole trader or partnership, they and their business are inseparable as they have unlimited liability (see Chapter 1.4.1) which means they are personally liable for any debts of the business.

A business may not be able to repay a loan or pay their suppliers and this may lead to closure of the business. Small businesses may find it difficult to repay loans as they have less retained profits, poor cash flows and fewer assets (items the business owns such as equipment, property and land).

A small business owner may also lack security because they have a limited product range so if a particular product does not achieve high sales the business has no alternative sources of income to support it.

A small business may only operate in one geographical area. If for example, a bakery, has branches in different parts of a town or city, a successful branch may be able to support a less successful branch. The business also gets wider recognition and can take advantage of bulk discounts for larger orders of supplies.

Large businesses often find it easier to pay suppliers and repay loans because they may own property and land, operate in many countries and therefore if part of the business runs into difficulties in one country this can be balanced by other parts of the business performing well. A business may be able to sell assets (things it owns), for example land and buildings, if it needs to raise funds. Large businesses have more security than small businesses.

Reward: Business success

The definition of success will vary according to the point of view of different stakeholders. Owners and shareholders are primarily concerned with earning a return on their investment whilst managers may focus on the prestige and kudos they can achieve. Rewards can also take the form of financial gain and fame. For example, Facebook co-founder Mark Zuckerberg's accumulated wealth is estimated to be $72 billion (£55bn) and is an easily recognisable figure in the media.

The criteria that might be used to judge success are as follows:

- **Sales growth** is usually a barometer of success as higher sales means a business is producing a product that is popular. A business with growing sales is likely to be experiencing an increasing market share and provided costs are kept under control rising profit should also follow.
- **Market share** shows the proportion of sales in the market made by the business. Firms attempt to grow their own market share at the expense of their rivals (see Chapter 2.1.1).

Reward: Profit

- **Profit levels** are the most common way a business will judge whether it has been successful. Marks & Spencer might make millions of pounds worth of profit before tax for its shareholders. However, it is important to look at that in the context of the amount of resources and capital employed. A sole trader that makes profit of £50,000 could argue they were more successful in terms of the average rate of return (see Chapter 2.4.1).
- **Customer satisfaction** is a real motivator for some businesses and the owners of these businesses might judge their success partly in the levels of positive customer feedback. Many small business owners, in particular, will take real pride in their work and receive a great deal of satisfaction from good reviews.
- **Dividends** are the share of the business' profit which is given out to shareholders. They are paid according to share volumes so the larger the shareholding the larger the dividend received. If, for example, Marks & Spencer decide to pay a 10p per share dividend then a shareholder with 100,000 shares would receive £10,000 in dividends. High dividend payments reflect large profits which may be as a result of effective management.
- **Job creation** might be seen as a measurement of success. If a business is able to employ a large number of people it can reflect the large amount of output the business is producing and gives the company a large standing in the community and in the eyes of the government.
- **Social benefits** are important for some businesses. Elon Musk creates freeware for other businesses to use. He has been rewarded with profits and his net worth is $17 billion (£13.35bn). Businesses such as Lush the 'fresh handmade cosmetics' company donate large sums to charity each year, their products are sold using minimal packaging and are made of natural ingredients and therefore they try to minimise the impact they have on the environment.

Independence

- Entrepreneurs who start a business also enjoy the freedom independence brings. They are free to make decisions and can keep all rewards of their business. Ingvar Kamprad, the founder and owner of IKEA, wanted the business to remain independent and therefore not owned by shareholders and financial institutions. IKEA is owned by a foundation and its profits are reinvested, used for charitable purposes or retained in the business.

Exam style question

Lush the 'fresh handmade cosmetics' company was started in the 1970s in Poole in Dorset by Mark Constantine and Liz Weir who created their own natural products for hair and skin. After successfully selling products to the Body Shop for many years they set up another venture of their own called Cosmetics-To-Go, a mail order cosmetics company which unfortunately was unsuccessful and failed. The failure of the business was due to overspending and trying to expand too quickly in the early stages of its life. What was left of the business including the name and product formulae was bought by another small business in Poole and several years later Mark and Liz and the owners of Cosmetics-To-Go got together and started to make and sell handmade products for hair and skin from a small shop in Poole. The name Lush was given to the new venture. In 1996, two Canadians came across the shop on a trip to England and decided that they wanted to open a similar shop in Vancouver, Canada. There are now approximately 105 Lush shops in the UK and more than 900 stores in 50 countries around the world. Lush are fierce advocates against animal cruelty and make donations to charities every year.

Questions

1. Identify the reasons for the failure of Cosmetics-To-Go. *(2 marks)*
2. Describe valuable lessons which were learnt from the failure of Cosmetics-To-Go which led to the success of Lush. *(4 marks)*
3. Identify and explain the rewards the owners of Lush have gained from their business? *(6 marks)*

Chapter review questions

1. Explain the risks associated with starting a business.
2. What is the most common reason for business failure?
3. Explain why business failure is very common.
4. Explain why a small business may lack security.
5. State three rewards which may be earned by business owners.
6. Identify three measures of business success.

Key terms

Customer satisfaction refers to how happy the customer is with the quality of service received.

Dividends are the share of the profits of a company, paid out to shareholders (owners of a business).

Financial security occurs when a business owner has assets or a person who can support them financially if they have difficulties repaying loans or money owed to suppliers.

Rewards are the returns a business owner can expect from a business and include: business success, profit and independence.

Risks are the negatives situations that may arise as a result of starting a business and they include: business failure, financial loss and lack of security.

Social benefits arise when business activity generates positive benefits for society.

Chapter 1.1.3

The role of business enterprise

Aims

By the end of this chapter, students should be able to understand:

- the role of business enterprise and the purpose of business activity.
- the role of entrepreneurship.

Role of business enterprise: to produce goods and services

Business organisations exist to produce either goods or services and in some cases both. Apple produces hardware and software, for example, in the form of smartphones and FaceTime. Amazon makes Kindles and provides an online shopping platform.

Hairdressers provide services to customers: haircuts, blow-dries, styling, colouring and in some cases produce hair products. For example, Vidal Sassoon and Toni & Guy make a range of hair products which are sold around the world.

Role of business enterprise: to meet customer needs

Business are either product or market oriented and most goods and services produced are **market oriented**, which means they are designed to take into account the needs and wants of consumers. It is important for businesses to make market orientated products and services so that they satisfy their customers, retain loyal customers and keep up with competitors.

Examples of market orientated products include water bottles with handles designed to be carried by athletes, disposable toothbrushes for use on airplanes, training shoes designed for different sports and gluten-free pasta and bread. Maclaren, a designer and manufacturer of pushchairs for babies and toddlers, constantly upgrade their products to adapt to the needs of customers and fend off competition.

Maclaren Triumph pushchair.

Product orientation

Product orientation occurs when a business designs and makes a product which it hopes will be attractive to consumers. Innovative and high-tech products are often product oriented.

Businesses which have a popular brand name often design and produce products that people buy because they are attracted to the brand name. For example, when Apple introduced the iPad it could be argued that it sold well because of the reputation Apple has for creating innovative products. It can also be argued that the iPad was Apple's response to consumers wanting to watch movies or read e-books on a screen larger than a smartphone. According to some sources Apple had already created the iPad many years before its launch in 2010 and therefore the iPad could be considered to be product oriented.

Other examples of product oriented goods include equipment and machinery made for other producers, e.g. tools for carpenters, equipment and machinery for farmers, medical equipment for use by doctors and surgeons when performing operations and medical procedures.

Role of business enterprise:
To add value (convenience, branding, quality, design, unique selling points)

Customers pay a particular price over and above the cost of production as it provides added value. Added value refers to the difference between the value of the inputs (factors of production) and that of the finished good or service. Added value = Value of the finished good or service – Value of the inputs (raw materials + labour + production process).

Businesses add value to products and services in a variety of ways:

1. **Convenience** – many firms try to respond to consumers' desires for convenient products. Examples include supermarkets selling vegetables which have been peeled and chopped, cans of tuna fish already combined with mayonnaise, or travel sized deodorants, shampoos and other toiletries.
2. **Branding** – consumers are often willing to pay higher prices for branded products. Supermarkets own brands are cheaper than branded food producers as customers believe that branded products are better quality then non-branded products. A Samsung smartphone will be more expensive than an unknown brand with similar product specifications.
3. **Quality** – products made with better quality materials tend to have higher prices. For example, a wardrobe made from chipboard from IKEA will be cheaper than a wardrobe made from solid oak.
4. **Design** – a custom-made birthday cake, piece of clothing or furniture is likely to be more expensive than a mass produced item. Value is added because of the personal input of the producer and increased time taken to produce the item. A higher level of skill may be necessary to make the good. Some producers use their unique designs as selling points. Bang and Olufsen produce audio equipment which have a unique physical design so some consumers are willing to pay more for design over functionality. Other people would choose a brand which is possibly less aesthetically pleasing but has outstanding audio quality, such as Onkyo.
5. **Unique selling point** – some businesses try to differentiate their products from others by offering something others do not have, such as restaurants where you eat in the dark, fridges with built in ice makers and door locks which open with a thumb print.

The role of entrepreneurship

To produce a good or service a business needs to use the factors of production in varying proportions. The four factors of production are:

Capital – manufactured resources e.g. machinery, tools and equipment.

Enterprise – the skills of a business person required to successfully combine the other factors of production.

Labour – the human resources e.g. skilled and unskilled labour.

Land – the natural resources e.g. oil, coal, wood and agricultural products.

The first letter of each of the 4 factors of production spells the word CELL. This is a useful way of remembering the factors of production.

An entrepreneur:

1. Organises resources (the four factors of production) to make products and/or services.
2. Makes decisions about what to produce, how to produce it and for whom to produce it in response to changing business conditions and needs and wants of consumers.
3. Takes risks because all business decisions have an element of risk as they may not lead to success and the desired result (see Chapter 1.1.2).

Exam style question 1

Salvador wants to set up a business and is seeking advice about the type of product or service he should sell.

Identify the ways in which the following businesses have added value to their products/service:

(a) Nike training shoes.

(b) A supermarket selling ready meals.

(c) A wedding dress made by a well-known designer.

(d) A camera made in Japan.

(e) A seller of electronic products which offers excellent after sales service.

(f) A self-service restaurant where food passes a customer on a conveyor belt. *(6 marks)*

Chapter review questions

1. Identify three reasons why business decisions come about.
2. Identify two ways that entrepreneurs come up with business ideas.
3. Describe possible risks of setting up a business.
4. Describe possible rewards from setting up a business.
5. Identify and give examples of ways businesses add value to products and services.
6. Identify the main roles of entrepreneurship.

Key terms

Added value is the difference between the value of the inputs (factors of production) and finished good or service.

Branding is when a business has a well-known brand name, image or reputation.

Capital describes the manufactured resources needed in a business e.g. machinery, tools, equipment, computers.

Enterprise describes the skills required by a business person to successfully combine the other factors of production.

Factors of production refer to the four categories of resources required for the production of goods and provision of services: capital, enterprise, land and labour.

Labour describes the human resources required in a business e.g. skilled and unskilled labour.

Land describes the natural resources required in a business e.g. oil, coal, wood and agricultural products.

Chapter 1.2.1

Customer needs

Aims

By the end of this chapter, students should be able to identify and understand:

- what customer needs are: price, quality, choice, and convenience.
- the importance of identifying and understanding customers: generating sales, business survival.

What are customer needs?

When deciding which product or service to buy in a competitive business environment, customers base their decision making on various factors. Imagine trying to decide which restaurant to go to for a birthday meal. Possibly the most influential factor would be the **price** as customers have an idea how much they are able and willing to spend on the good or service. Associated with the price of a product is the **quality** of a product or service. It is not always the case that higher prices mean better quality, but there is a relationship between price and quality and this would be taken into consideration when choosing between restaurants. It is sometimes difficult to assess the quality of food in a restaurant before trying it and therefore customers increasingly rely on customer reviews which can be found on the internet.

It is not always the case that higher prices mean better quality, but there is a relationship between price and quality.

Customers like to have a **choice** of restaurants and often in competitive markets (where there is a large choice for consumers) businesses respond by using non-price factors to attract customers. Examples include: loyalty cards, free gifts, excellent customer service, gift wrapping, reliability, efficiency, and other unique selling points.

Convenience takes many forms. Examples include: 24 hour supermarkets, home deliveries for shopping (once customers spend over a certain amount), online shopping, and restaurants using delivery services such as Deliveroo.

Case study: factors which influence choice of trainers (sports shoes)

Price – What is your budget? Are you going to buy the latest design in trainers, which will be more expensive than an older style?

Quality – Do you need trainers which are going to last a long time because you wear them often or play a specialist sport? Are you going to purchase trainers which are mass produced or specialist trainers for example for long distance running? Are you happy to purchase trainers of lower quality for casual wear?

Choice – Do you enjoy having many styles, colours and designs to choose from or does too much choice overwhelm you? Do you enjoy looking for trainers which are different in design from popular styles or do you like to have trainers which are similar to those of others?

Convenience – Do you like to shop online and spend time looking for trainers on websites such as Sports Direct or do you like to visit shops and try on trainers before buying? Do you prefer to visit shops to purchase the trainers or are you happy to wait for your online delivery?

The importance of identifying and understanding customer needs

Businesses exist to satisfy customer needs and wants so that customers will purchase their goods and services and generate **sales revenues** which will cover costs, make a profit and ensure **business survival** (see Chapter 1.3.1).

Case study

A new takeaway restaurant called Poulet Rotisserie opened in Leeds City centre. It sells whole chickens cooked on a rotisserie along with accompaniments such as salads and roast potatoes. It also sells a selection of cakes and other desserts. The shop has a few small tables where customers can choose to eat in the shop instead of taking away. It is aimed at people wanting to pick up cooked food on their way home from work or for people to buy when entertaining guests at home and also offers catering for parties. The chickens are cooked with a range of flavours: chilli, traditional and Cajun.

To survive Poulet Rotisserie needs to generate sales. It faces stiff competition from major supermarkets which also sell cooked chickens, salads and food for parties and entertaining. Poulet Rotisserie charges higher prices for its products than supermarkets because it is producing on a much smaller scale and cannot take advantage of economies of scale. It tries to ensure that its chickens and accompaniments are better in quality and offer a greater choice than those found in supermarkets. The opportunity for customers to eat in the shop is another method of generating sales. Poulet Rotisserie also offers free delivery for orders above £50.

Poulet Rotisserie is finding it difficult to compete with supermarkets despite getting positive publicity in local newspapers. Business during the week tends to be quiet and most of their orders for catering services occurs at the weekend. They are considering trying to break into the lunchtime market for office workers by offering a roast dinner takeaway and delivery service to generate sales and ensure survival.

Exam style questions

1. Outline the customers' needs that Poulet Rotisserie has identified. *(4 marks)*
2. State two ways in which Poulet Rotisserie has tried to differentiate itself from its competitors. *(2 marks)*
3. Analyse the decision of Poulet Rotisserie to offer a roast dinner takeaway and delivery service. *(6 marks)*

Chapter review questions

1. Identify the four needs of customers.
2. Give examples of each of the four main customer needs when considering at which supermarket to buy groceries.
3. Describe the main reasons a business has for satisfying customer needs.

Key terms

Business survival – when a business manages to generate sales sufficient to cover costs in the short term (near future) and in the longer term to cover costs and create profits.

Choice – the number of similar goods or services available in a market for the customer to choose from.

Convenience – the ease with which the customer can purchase and use or experience the good or service.

Price – monetary cost of the good or service to the customer.

Quality – the product or service is value for money, of a good standard and fit for the purpose intended.

Chapter 1.2.2

Market research

Aims

By the end of this chapter students should be able to understand:

- the purpose of market research.
- the various methods of market research.
- the role of data in market research.

The purpose of market research

Market research is the process of gathering, analysing and presenting information about a specific market, its customers and market trends. It provides information for decision-making because the business has a fuller understanding of its market.

Market research is carried out for 4 main reasons:

1. To identify and understand consumer needs.
Market research has helped low cost airlines such as Ryanair to develop a new type of airline that focuses on a 'no frills' model. Surveying their passengers helped the firm to design a highly profitable service which prioritises low fares and convenience over extras like complimentary food and drink.

2. To identify gaps in the market
Nando's have undertaken thorough market research when identifying new sites for their ambitious expansion program of the last few years. It is important to assess whether a town or a district has sufficient demand for the casual dining experience they offer and to take the existing level of competition into account before investing in setting up a new restaurant.

3. To reduce risk
Any new business venture carries an element of risk. Apple invested a lot of money into developing and launching their iPad range of tablet computers. Carrying out a range of different types of market research such as surveys and product testing will have provided them with a degree of confidence that it was a risk worth taking and the products have proved a success.

4. To inform business decisions
Businesses decisions such as the decision from PureGym to invest heavily in new sites would have been made in the context of market research which suggested a growing appetite among UK fitness enthusiasts for a pay-as-you-go gym model which didn't lock customers into long and expensive contracts. The owners of PureGym will have found the decision making process more straightforward with the benefit of extensive market research that backed their business model.

Hence, market research is essential for a business to gain a competitive advantage over its rivals because it enables the business to adapt to changing market trends. However, market research can have its limitations, such as biased (unrepresentative) findings and outdated information being used to draw conclusions.

Market research can also be categorised as **primary research** (new data that has yet to be collected for a specific purpose) or as **secondary research** (data that has already been collected by someone else).

Primary research

Primary research is the gathering of data that does not already exist, i.e. it is the collection of new and original data. It is not usually possible to collect data from every existing or potential customer (known as the **population**). Therefore, businesses use **sampling methods** to get statistically valid results from a portion of the population (known as a **sample**).

There are numerous methods of primary research, including:

- **Questionnaires** – These are paper-based surveys, such as ones conducted by an interviewer or sent in the post for people to respond. Hotels often use questionnaires to get feedback from their customers.
- **Online surveys** – Similar to questionnaires, online surveys make use of email or the internet to conduct primary research. These have grown in popularity as they are cheaper and faster than questionnaires.
- **Interviews** – This involves an interviewer asking individuals a series of questions. The two main forms are 'face-to-face interviews' (conducting the research in the presence of the interviewees) and telephone interviews (using telecommunications to conduct the interviews).
- **Observations** – This method involves the business observing and recording *what* people do and *how* people behave, e.g. observing shopping habits of customers in a supermarket.
- **Focus groups** (also known as **consumer panels**) – This involves asking in-depth questions to a small group of people (the panel) when a business wants to gauge opinions about a product, forecast market trends or launch a new product.
- **Test marketing** – This involves experiments being conducted in selected areas to test the response of customers before launching a product on a mass scale. To launch a new product is often very expensive, so test marketing helps a business to reduce risks of launching unsuccessful products.

The advantages of primary research include:

- Relevant data is collected for the specific needs of the business.
- Up-to-date information is gathered.
- Uniqueness of the data as no one else has collected it.
- Confidentiality can exist as no one else has access to the primary data that has been collected.
- Control over what and how data is collected is improved as the researcher can decide on requirements such as the sampling method and the timeframe of the research.
- **Closed questions** in interviews and surveys have definite answers (such as 'yes/no' or 'male/female') so makes it relatively easy to aggregate the results of the respondents.
- **Open questions** allow businesses to gain insight to the views and opinions of respondents by allowing them to develop their answers (such as 'Why do you prefer to buy…?').

The disadvantages of primary research include:

- Time-consuming processes of primary data collection and analysis (it is usually quicker to use secondary data sources).
- Expensive as the information is not readily available, e.g. the cost of hiring interviewers and conducting focus group meetings.
- Validity of the primary data might be questioned, such as:
  - the chosen sample size might be too small, so results are not representative.
  - the sampling method used might introduce bias, again reducing the validity of any findings.
  - poor research design, e.g. poorly worded questionnaires.
  - the possibility that research data becomes outdated by the time the investigation is completed.

Secondary research

Secondary research involves the collection and analysis of information that already exists. The information can come from internal sources (such as company annual reports and corporate websites) or from external sources (such as news media, government economic data and market review websites).

Secondary research methods:

- **Internet** – There is a wealth of information on the internet that a business can use to find out about their market. A restaurant planning to open in a certain area can go to websites like OpenTable to get a sense of the needs and wants of the local consumers.

- **Market reports** – market reports are reports produced by businesses and consumer watchdogs to provide information about what is happening in a particular market. For example, an estate agent can easily find house price reports from lenders like Halifax to get an idea of key market trends in their region.
- **Government reports** – the Office for National Statistics (ONS) reports regularly on a wide range of metrics that can be vital for businesses trying to find out more about their target market. For example, the number of households in an area or demographic changes such as the level of immigration.

The advantages of secondary research include:

- Cheaper and less time-consuming to collect as the information has already been gathered by someone else.
- Faster access to data as the information can be readily available, such as company information and data available on the World Wide Web.
- More accessibility, e.g. the internet has improved access and opportunities to conduct secondary research.

The disadvantages of secondary research include:

- Outdated information (because the information is not new) means there is little value to the business.
- Incomplete data is likely to exist as the secondary data was originally collected for a different purpose.
- As there is potentially so much secondary data, much of the information might prove to be irrelevant or inappropriate for the purpose of the business.
- Widely available data means that rival companies also have access to the secondary data, thereby reducing any competitive advantage that the business might have.

The use of data in market research: Qualitative and quantitative research

Market research can be categorised as either qualitative or quantitative. **Qualitative research** seeks to understand how and why people behave in a certain way, such as why some consumers might prefer an iPhone over a Samsung mobile phone. Examples of qualitative research include in-depth interviews, focus groups and observations.

Quantitative research involves the use of numerical and quantifiable data, such as a company's own financial records and official government statistics. It is often used to establish trends (such as rising demand for wearable technology) and relationships (such as the correlation between consumer income and the demand for cars).

Social media

The increasing use of social media has provided many different types of businesses with the opportunity to find out more about their market. Twitter might allow a budding entrepreneur to search for other companies that are in a market and make judgements about the strengths and weaknesses of their brand and their product or service. Instagram and Facebook contain billions of consumers giving detailed feedback (often with photographic evidence) on their consumption of goods and services. This information can be used by businesses to tailor their products to the wants and needs of an increasingly discerning and well-informed consumer.

The reliability of market research data

Market research data may lead to a business taking a significant change of direction. It might be that a new pricing strategy is adopted, or perhaps a significant investment is made into the research and development of a new type of product. If the decision to take such risks is to be worthwhile then the business owners must have a high degree of confidence in the market research data. However, the reliability of the data that is being used to guide the business is often questionable. Reasons for data being flawed include biases due to not enough data being collected or due to interviewers asking leading questions.

A classic example of when a market research failure can cost a company millions was when Coca-Cola tried to change the taste of their drink in the 1980s. Focus group and product testing results were favourable and tens of millions were poured into the development and marketing of 'New Coke'. However, when the product did arrive in the shops it completely failed and the old flavour was quickly reinstated.

Exam style question 1

1. Which **two** of the following are examples of primary market research? *(2 marks)*
   (a) A café looking at the McDonald's website to assess their pricing and product range.
   (b) A home furnishing shop finding out the average rate of home ownership in their town from the local authority.
   (c) A clothing brand conducting a focus group with teens to assess responses to their new designs.
   (d) A Bed and Breakfast looking at their competitors' reviews on tripadvisor.com.
   (e) A call centre calling back customers to ask them about their view on the standard of customer service received.
2. Explain one advantage for a training company that uses social media as its main method of market research. *(3 marks)*
3. Explain one disadvantage to a business of relying solely on quantitative data in their market research. *(3 marks)*
4. Discuss the factors a small business owner should consider when deciding which type of market research to use. *(6 marks)*

Chapter review questions

1. What is meant by 'market research'?
2. Why is market research important to a business?
3. Distinguish between primary research and secondary research.
4. Distinguish between quantitative and qualitative research.
5. Outline the advantages and disadvantages of primary research.
6. Outline the advantages and disadvantages of secondary research.

Key terms

Market research is the process of gathering, analysing and presenting information about a specific market, its customers and market trends. It allows businesses to make more informed decisions.

Primary research (also known as **field research**) is the gathering of data that does not already exist, i.e. it is the collection of new data.

Qualitative research seeks to understand *how* and *why* people behave in a certain way through methods such as in-depth interviews, focus groups and observations.

Quantitative research involves the use of numerical and quantifiable data, such as financial records and government statistics, to establish market trends and relationships (correlation).

Secondary research (also known as **desk research**) involves the collection and analysis of information that already exists, from sources such as company annual reports, corporate websites and the news media.

Chapter 1.2.3

Market segmentation

Aims

By the end of this chapter, students should be able to understand:

- the meaning of market segmentation.
- how businesses use market segmentation to target customers by identifying: location, demographics, lifestyle, income, and age.
- market mapping to identify a gap in the market and the competition.

Market segments

Market segmentation occurs when a business divides the total market for a good or service into different parts (or segments) by grouping together individuals, organisations or families with similar characteristics. Examples of how businesses segment markets include:

Location

- By geographical area, for example: rural, urban or a particular region of the country.

  For example, supermarkets located near to a beach will stock more buckets, spades and water toys than a supermarket located in the countryside.

Demographics

- Ethnicity (e.g. African, Chinese, Asian, Caucasian, or Indian).
- Religion (e.g. Jewish, Christian, Rastafarian, or Muslim).

  Examples include: supermarkets selling a wide range of food products to cater for different cuisines and cultures. McDonald's in India makes burgers from pork and not beef to accommodate local culture and customs.

- Gender (male or female).

  Examples include: different colours or designs of training shoes to appeal to different genders. Coca-Cola launched Coke Zero, in a black can, to appeal to men and be an alternative to Coke Light (Diet Coke).

Lifestyle

- Lifestyle (e.g. outdoors, sports, music lover, animal lover, vegetarian, or train spotter).

  Examples include: clothing aimed at hikers, specialised camping equipment for serious campers, tents with floral designs for 'glampers' (people who enjoy glamorous camping), bags to carry yoga mats, waterproof bags for swimmers, and vegetarian options in restaurants. A magazine shop is a good example of market segmentation as it sells magazines to cater for a wide range of interests which include cooking, motorcycles, cars, trains, wine and beer making, photography, and interior design.

Income

- Income (e.g. unemployed, low income, middle income, and high income earners).
- Socio-economic groupings in a population divide people by occupation, e.g. unemployed, unskilled workers, skilled workers, and professionals.

  Examples include: retailers of designer clothing choosing to locate in an area where customers have high incomes, such as in Chelsea and Kensington in London. Factory outlets and discount stores may locate in areas with inhabitants with lower incomes or where land is readily available.

Age

- Age categories include: young children, teenagers and old age pensioners.

  Examples of goods and services aimed at different age groups include: indoor play centres for toddlers, ballet and art classes aimed at young children, tuition centres for GCSEs and A Level students, bingo halls, shops selling mobility scooters, and swimming lessons for adults.

Market mapping

Market mapping is a visual tool used to identify the competitors of a business and gaps in a market. A map of a market is created using chosen variables, for example, price and quality, to identify the position of businesses in a market. Other examples of variables used in market mapping include mass market versus niche market, and traditional versus fashionable.

The market map in Figure 1.2.3a shows restaurant chains in the UK, and indicates that there is a gap in the market for more high quality and reasonably priced restaurants. There are many restaurants in the medium quality and medium price range and therefore this part of the market is very competitive (or saturated). This market map may help a restaurant owner to decide which part of the market to target. On the other hand, the map may not be entirely accurate and be incomplete. Market and consumer preferences change all the time, so even though it looks as if there is currently a gap in the market this may not be the case when the new restaurant opens.

Figure 1.2.3a: Market map of restaurant chains in the UK

Advantages of market maps

- Market maps provide a visual image of the position of businesses in a market and may lead to decisions about where a new firm in a market should position themselves to fill a gap or take on competitors.
- A market map may help a business identify the key characteristics of a competitor and help them to design features that differentiate them from competition so they can attract more customers.

Disadvantages

- The map is based on opinions of the creator (although it can be based on market research of customers to gauge their perceptions) so may not be entirely accurate.
- The environment in which businesses operate is constantly changing and the popularity of products can change at any time. The map is static, and not necessarily an accurate picture of the market.

Exam style questions

1. Explain one advantage to a business of using a market map. *(3 marks)*
2. Explain one disadvantage to a business of using a market map. *(3 marks)*

Demographics are characteristics of a population of people which include: age, gender, ethnicity, nationality, or religion.

Chapter review questions

1. Outline three ways a market can be segmented, such as the market for digital cameras.
2. Why might businesses find market segmentation a useful tool?
3. Describe two reasons why a business may create a market map.
4. What are the limitations of using a market map to make business decisions?

Key terms

Demographics are characteristics of a population of people which include: age, gender, ethnicity, nationality, or religion.

Market mapping is a visual tool used to identify the competitors of a business and gaps in a market. It is created using chosen variables, for example, price and quality.

Market segmentation occurs when a business divides the total market for a product into different parts or segments by grouping together individuals, organisations or families with similar characteristics.

Socio-economic groups in a population segment people by occupation e.g. unemployed, unskilled worker, skilled worker, or professional.

Chapter 1.2.4

The competitive environment

Aims

By the end of this chapter, students should be able to understand:

- strengths and weaknesses of competitors based on: price, quality, location, product range and customer service.
- the impact of competition on business decision making.

The competitive environment

Businesses in the UK operate in a range of different markets characterised by very different levels of competition. The Eurostar service from London to Paris might seem like a monopoly provider (a single provider in a market) of train services on that route at first glance but it still has to compete for passengers in the face of competition from airlines and coach companies. This competition sets limitations on Eurostar in terms of their pricing and marketing strategy as well as the type of service they offer.

On the other hand, the market for car and van hire in the UK is very competitive and consists of multinationals such as Sixt but also a range of local providers. In addition, price comparison websites such as travelsupermarket.com can be used by consumers to ensure that they are getting a good deal. This forces the businesses in this market to focus on pricing in a competitive manner.

When a business is trying to find new business opportunities it is important to assess just how competitive the market for their product is. This is especially the case if the business is not offering an entirely new product or service. Business owners can and should carry out extensive market research (see Chapter 1.2.2) to investigate the number of other providers in the market place, the type of product that is being offered, the pricing strategies adopted and the needs and wants of customers.

Assessing the strengths and weaknesses of competitors based on the following variables

Price – Stelios Haji-Ioannou founded the Easyjet airline in the 1990s as a low-cost alternative to established 'flag carriers' such as British Airways and Iberia. Stelios correctly identified a huge potential market for leisure and business travellers who were prepared to accept a 'no-frills' service in order to travel at a cheaper price. Stelios and Michael O'Leary's Ryanair spotted a weakness in the pricing strategies of their competitors which has changed the face of modern air travel and forced prices (and some would say standards) down in the industry.

Quality – Hawksmoor is a chain of high-end steak restaurants in the UK. When it was established by Will Beckett and Huw Gott in 2006 they wanted to position it as a high quality restaurant that was different to the steak restaurants that already existed in the capital. Evaluating the quality of service and food that was offered by existing restaurants in the premium space would have been central to devising a menu and environment that could capture market share. Hawksmoor now has several restaurants in the UK and an outpost in Manhattan.

Location – In retail, a good location can be a great competitive advantage. However, those businesses that have been quick to spot new trends such as the 'out of town' shopping boom can gain a competitive advantage over firms that are stuck in the High Street (town centre). Having the right unit in a shopping centre can have a big impact. Research has shown that units that are near lifts or the main entrance can expect to entice more shoppers than those deep inside the shopping centre. Bars and restaurants will also need to compete robustly for the right locations in order to guarantee plenty of passing trade.

Product range – Established businesses might leave a gap in their product range which, if spotted, can offer a new entrant into a market an opportunity to gain significant market share. A good example here is the rise in gluten-free or vegan variations of popular foodstuffs. New, smaller businesses have been able to enter such markets where established food companies had failed to develop their product range to cater to these tastes.

Customer service – Sports Direct and Poundland are two prominent High Street (town centre) retailers that regularly receive poor reviews for their customer service. Such low service standards could help a new entrant into the sportswear market in a locality to thrive because offering superior standards of service could be used to gain a competitive edge.

The impact of competition on business decision making

The more competitive the market that a business operates in, the more aware it must be of what the competitor response is likely to be to their business decisions. A business that is launching a new type of product might be tempted to use skim pricing (see page 83). However, it will be aware that the initial high price could provide competitors with an incentive to launch rival products. This happens in technological markets when firms produce new hardware and software. An example would be the use of fingerprint technology in smartphones. When Apple pioneered the use of this technology it provided a USP (unique selling point) that enabled them to charge a high price. However, such technology has now been adopted by Samsung and other smartphone manufacturers.

Businesses in competitive markets may have to charge a competitive price and focus on customer service to gain an edge. Review websites and comments on Facebook pages can make or break a small business. Such firms are therefore forced to attend to their training and recruitment methods to ensure that a positive and friendly outlook is maintained. Monopoly markets with a single dominant firm may decide to focus on maximising profits for shareholders by setting prices high. This might be a profitable strategy but businesses must accept the risk of high prices attracting new competitors into the market.

Exam style question 1

1. Explain one disadvantage for business of operating in a competitive environment. *(3 marks)*
2. A new pizza delivery service plans to open up in Birmingham. Discuss how the competitive environment is likely to impact on its decisions with regard to its marketing mix. *(6 marks)*

Chapter review questions

1. Explain why a firm has to be aware of and ready to respond to changes in:
   (a) the pricing strategies of competitors.
   (b) the quality of competitors' product or service.
   (c) the location of competitors.
   (d) the product range of competitors.
   (e) the customer service standards offered by competitors.
2. Explain how and why a business must consider the response of its competitors to its decisions.
3. Explain two examples of businesses that have had to take their competitors into account when making business decisions.

Key terms

Competitive environment refers to the level of and type of competition a business faces in a market.

Chapter 1.3.1

Business aims and objectives

Aims

By the end of this chapter, students should be able to understand:

- the meaning of business aims and objectives.
- financial and non-financial business aims and objectives when starting up.
- why aims and objectives differ between businesses.

Business aims and objectives

All business organisations should have clear aims and objectives. **Aims** define the purpose of a business and what it hopes to achieve in the long term. **Objectives** are the short to medium term goals or targets that businesses intend to achieve. Aims are broken down into objectives. For example, an aim of a business may be to become more environmentally friendly. An objective might be to reduce waste by using only recyclable packaging.

Aims and objectives provide managers and employees with a sense of direction regarding where the business wants to be. Without clear aims and objectives, organisations do not know where they are headed and this can have disastrous effects in the long run (including business failure). Objectives also allow managers to measure and control business activity. Furthermore, clear objectives can help to unite employees who share a common goal.

Professor Peter F. Drucker devised the concept of **SMART objectives**. He suggested that all objectives should be clearly formulated using this framework, so that objectives are:

- **Specific** – Objectives should be concise and clear.
- **Measurable** – Objectives should be quantifiable.
- **Achievable** – Objectives should be attainable.
- **Realistic** – Objectives should be sensible and practical.
- **Time restricted** – Objectives should be attainable within a given time period.

An example of a SMART objective for McDonald's might be "to achieve 10% sales growth in China within the next two years."

Financial aims and objectives

Businesses have a variety of financial aims and objectives. These include:

- **Survival** – This is one of the main objectives for all businesses. Whilst survival is clearly an important objective for new businesses, it also applies to established businesses trading in turbulent times of an economic recession. To survive in the long run, businesses need to at least break-even (see Chapter 1.3.2).

- **Profit** – Businesses can only survive if they are profitable. For the owners, profit also represents a source of income. A sole trader (see Chapter 1.4.1) can keep all the profit for personal use, whereas the profit earned by a company is distributed to shareholders (the owners) and/or retained to be used by the business. Public sector organisations are less likely to aim to make a profit, although any surplus made can be used as a source of finance to fund their operation.

- **Sales** – For some businesses, their main objective is to maximise sales revenue as they may wish to sell as many products as possible to become the market leader. IKEA aims to make their products affordable to many people, so low cost pricing allows them to maximise sales revenue.

- **Market share** – This is a key measure of an organisation's growth. Market share is calculated by expressing a firm's sales revenue as a percentage of the industry's total sales revenue. The **growth** of an organisation tends to lead to greater market share. Having higher market share has several benefits, such as the ability to enjoy economies of scale, strong customer loyalty and being more competitive.
- **Financial security** – All businesses aim to be financially secure which means that their assets (what the business owns) are greater than their liabilities (what the business owes). If a business is financially secure they can pay off their debts using their assets and they have sufficient cash flow (see Chapter 1.3.3) to cover their day-to-day-expenses.

Non-financial aims and objectives

- **Social objectives** – These are objectives which aim to solve social issues or provide benefits to society. All profits of the business are used to fund projects for the wider benefit of society and not just to reward the owners of the business. In such cases, the profits are donated to charities or used to fund projects in the community.

Increasingly, businesses are becoming socially responsible and are contributing to society by, for example, sponsoring charitable and sporting events and making charitable donations. They may provide work experience placements and act as mentors for students in schools and colleges, thereby enabling students to gain valuable skills.

Some businesses, such as Divine Chocolate and Taylors of Harrogate, operate using principles of fair trade and thereby agree to pay their suppliers a fair price for their products. This helps to increase wealth and prosperity in the communities where the suppliers are located, usually in less economically developed countries.

Case study

Social Bites is a social enterprise which donates all profits to charity. It is a café which has five branches in Scotland. Customers can buy a meal, online or in person, for a homeless person. The meal is given to a person when they enter the café. A quarter of the staff employed are homeless people and they open the cafés in the evening to feed homeless people and provide them with support and assistance with the aim of getting them out of the cycle of being homeless (http://social-bite.co.uk/).

- **Personal satisfaction** – A small business owner may enjoy the satisfaction gained from running their own business. For example, an architect who worked for a large multinational practice decides to set up a practice of their own and derives great personal satisfaction from working for themself, being the main decision maker and being independent.
- **Challenge** – A challenge to produce a particular good or service may be an aim for a business. It could be a personal challenge for a small business owner to set up, for example a pottery studio, hairdressers, restaurant, or to create a brand of trousers (www.hebtro.co).
- **Independence** – Aims and objectives of sole traders, partnerships and small limited liability companies (see Chapter 1.4.1) may be to be independent and to enjoy the freedom to make their own decisions.
- **Control** – A business owner (such as a sole trader or partner) may enjoy the control they have over their business and ability to make day-to-day decisions and decisions about the long term future of the organisation.

Control, independence and challenge are all aims that may be shared by small business owners.

Why aims and objectives differ between businesses

Businesses are like people and each one has its own unique personality and characteristics and therefore every business has slightly different aims and objectives. To survive, all businesses must make a profit but how they make the profits and what they choose to do with them differs between businesses.

A sole trader (see Chapter 1.4.1) with a new business might set survival as the main objective, whereas a franchise might decide that growth is its key business objective.

As a business grows, it is likely to move away from being a sole trader to a partnership or private limited company. Thus, its business objectives are also likely to change. For example, many limited liability companies will aim for profit maximisation by operating in overseas markets.

Ziferblat (www.ziferblat.co.uk) is a shared meeting space, café, work space or somewhere you can meet friends and play board games. It charges customers £0.08 per minute and everything else in the space is free. Customers help themselves to drinks and refreshments. Although Ziferblat may aim to be profitable they also may wish to be market leaders in shared work and leisure space with a unique pricing strategy.

Exam style question 1

Identify and explain a possible financial and non-financial aim of the following businesses:

(a) A café which is designed to be like a 1930s tea room. *(4 marks)*

(b) A tuition centre offering support to GCSE, A Level and BTEC students after school. *(4 marks)*

(c) A horse riding school which extends its lessons to students with special individual needs. *(4 marks)*

(d) An estate agent established by a person who once worked for a large estate agent with *branches* across the UK. *(4 marks)*

Chapter review questions

1. Outline why it is important for businesses to have objectives.
2. Identify possible financial objectives of a business.
3. Explain why survival is an important business objective.
4. Explain why profitability is important to businesses.
5. Explain what is meant by financial security.
6. Explain the benefits of increasing market share.
7. Identify possible non-financial aims of a small business.
8. Explain why aims and objectives differ between businesses.

Key terms

Aims are the purpose of a business and what it hopes to achieve in the long term.

Objectives are the short to medium term targets of a business organisation, e.g. survival, growth, market share, wealth creation and profitability.

SMART objectives provide a framework for setting objective targets that are: specific, measurable, achievable, realistic and time constrained.

Social objectives are objectives which aim to solve social issues or provide benefits to society.

Survival is where a business aims to survive in the short term and into the long term by increasing sales, attempting to minimise costs, increasing market share and keeping abreast with competition.

Chapter 1.3.2

Business revenues, costs and profit

Aims

By the end of this chapter, students should be able to understand:

- the concept and calculation of revenue, costs and profit.
- break even diagrams.

Revenue

Revenue is the money coming into a business from the sale of goods and/or services. Revenue is often referred to as **sales revenue** or **sales turnover**. The formula for calculating sales revenue is:

Revenue = Price x Quantity sold

For example, if a business charges an average price of £30 for each pair of its shoes and manages to sell 120 pairs in a week, its total sales revenue will be £3,600 (i.e. £30 x 120).

Costs

Costs are items of expenditure incurred by a business. Examples include: wages and salaries to employees, rent for business premises, payments for raw materials, fuel and other bills, advertising expenses and taxes to the government. Costs are not easy to control, especially in larger organisations. Businesses must pay careful attention to their costs to maintain a good cash flow position; otherwise they can run into liquidity problems (see Chapter 1.3.3). Costs can be classified in several ways: fixed, variable and total costs.

1. **Fixed costs** – These are costs that have to be paid regardless of how much the business produces or sells. For example, management salaries and rent have to be paid irrespective of how much a business sells or produces.

Figure 1.3.2a: Fixed costs chart for a business with £2,000 fixed costs

2. **Variable costs** – These are costs that change as the level of output increases. For example, raw material costs and wage payments will increase if a textiles firm makes more curtains.

Figure 1.3.2b: Variable costs chart for a business

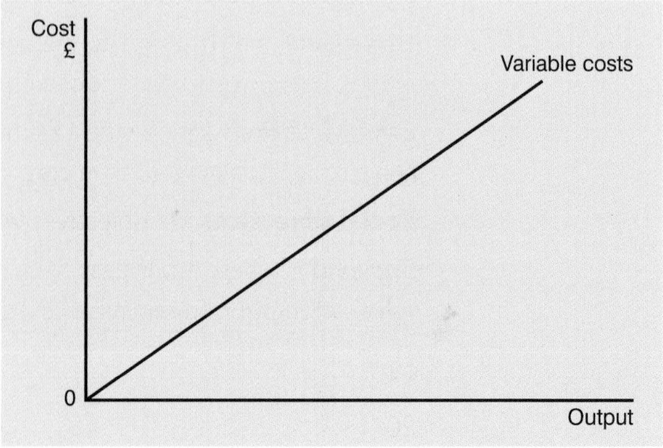

3. **Total costs** – This is the sum of all fixed costs and all variable costs. Total costs, shown in Figure 1.3.2c, start at the same level of fixed costs – if nothing is produced, fixed costs still have to be paid.

Total Costs = Fixed Costs + Variable Costs

Figure 1.3.2c: Total costs chart for a business

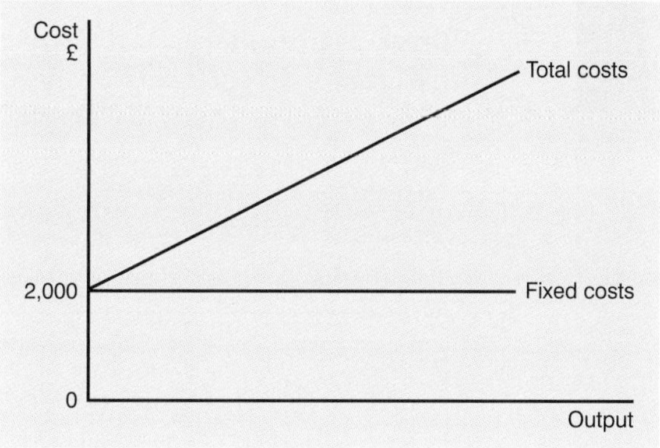

Profit

A business earns **profit** if its revenues exceed its total costs. Thus, profit can be calculated as:

Profit = Sales revenue – Total costs

A business earns a **loss** if its total costs exceed its total revenues.

Exam style question 1

Complete the information in the table below. *(3 marks)*

Units sold (shoes)	Sales Revenue (£)	Total Fixed Costs (£)	Total Variable Costs (£)	Total Costs (£)	Profit/Loss (£)
0	0	4,200	0	4,200	(4,200)
60	3,600	4,200	1,500	5,700	
120	7,200	4,200	3,000	7,200	
180	10,800	4,200	4,500		2,100

N.B. Figure in brackets refers to a loss

Interest

Interest is the cost of borrowing money or the reward for saving. The effective rate of interest on a loan would be calculated as follows:

Interest rate = Interest paid/amount borrowed x 100

Here is an example:

A café owner borrows £24,000 to set up a new branch of their café. It is a one year loan and is therefore paid back in 12 instalments. If each repayment is £2,100 per month, then the total repaid would be £25,200. We can deduct the amount of money borrowed from that total in order to find the interest paid:

£25,200 – £24,000 = £1,200

We then calculate the interest paid as a % of the amount borrowed:

£1,200/£24,000 = 0.05 or 5%

Break-even and the interpretation of break-even diagrams

Break-even analysis is a tool used to identify the output level where sales revenues equal total costs. At the **break-even point**, no profit or loss is made. Many new businesses strive to break-even as part of their organisational objectives (see Chapter 2.1.2). The formula to calculate the break-even level of output is:

$$\textbf{Break-even quantity} = \frac{\textbf{Fixed costs}}{\textbf{Selling Price – Variable cost per unit}}$$

Take the following as a numerical example for Ashworth Shoes Ltd.:

Fixed costs	=	£1,600 per month
Variable costs	=	£20 per pair of shoes
Selling price	=	£60 per pair of shoes

The break-even quantity can be calculated as: £1,600 / (£60 – £20) = 40 pairs of shoes per month. We can check that Ashworth Shoes Ltd. breaks even at 40 pairs of shoes each month by comparing total sales revenues with total costs:

Sales revenues	=	£60 x 40	=	£2,400 per month
Total costs	=	£1,600 + (£20 x 40)	=	£2,400 per month

This information can be presented in a **break-even chart**:

Figure 1.3.2d: Break-even chart for Ashworth Shoes Ltd.

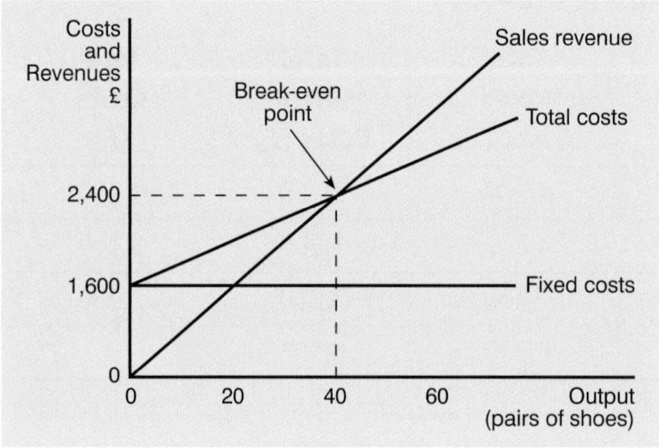

Any sales made beyond the break-even point (i.e. revenues exceed costs) means that the business earns a profit. This can be shown in a break-even chart by measuring the vertical difference between sales revenues and total costs at each level of output:

Figure 1.3.2e: Break-even chart showing profit and loss

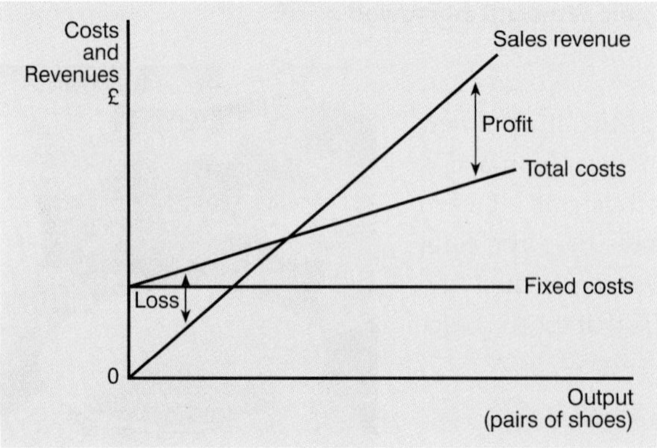

A break-even chart can also be used to show the **margin of safety** (**MOS**). This is the numerical difference between a firm's level of demand and the break-even quantity. It shows how 'safe' the business is in terms of exceeding the amount needed to break-even.

The amount of sales a business is making in excess of the break-even point is known as its **margin of safety**.

Margin of safety = Level of output – Break-even point

For example, if Ashworth Shoes Ltd. expects to sell 60 pairs of shoes each week, then its margin of safety is 20 pairs of shoes (60–40 pairs of shoes).

Figure 1.3.2f: The margin of safety for Ashworth Shoes Ltd.

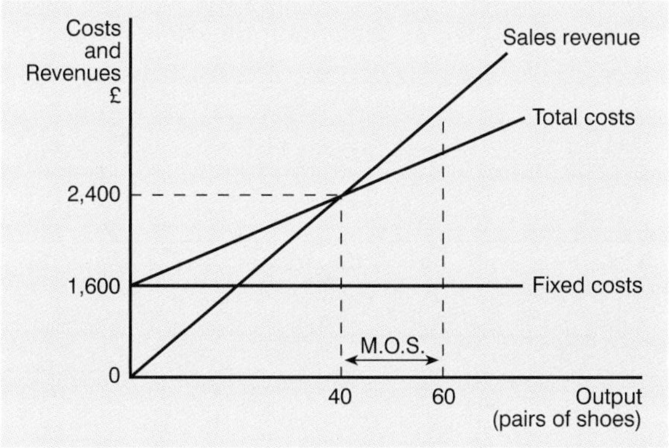

Exam style question 2

In-a-Box is an online business which is planning to make plastic stationery boxes to sell to schools and offices. In-a-Box wants to know how many stationery boxes it needs to sell to break-even. The cost and revenue data for In-a-Box is shown below.

- Fixed costs are £2,000 per month.
- Variable costs are £20 per box.
- In-a-Box wants to produce 80 boxes per month.
- Selling price of each box is £60.

(a) Use the information above to calculate the break-even level of output for In-a-Box. *(2 marks)*

(b) Calculate the margin of safety for In-a-Box if they produce 80 boxes in a month. *(2 marks)*

Break-even: the impact of changes in revenue and costs

Break-even diagrams are useful as a visual tool to assess the likely profitability of a business and, importantly, as a means through which to assess the impact of changes in certain variables. For example, a rise in the rental charged to a business for its premises or a change in the cost of raw materials would increase the level of sales required to reach break-even.

- A rise in the fixed costs of production will raise the break-even level of output.
- A fall in the variable costs of production will reduced the break-even level of output.
- Increasing the price of a product will reduce the break-even level of output (but a higher price can mean it becomes harder to sell the product).

Firms may also wish to gauge the impact of a change in their pricing strategy on the level of sales required to break even. For example, raising prices will allow firms to cover all costs more quickly but this will have implications for the total level of sales that they are able to make. Conversely, reducing prices may encourage demand for a product but the firm may not wish to risk increasing the break-even level of sales.

Analysis of break-even diagrams can allow entrepreneurs or investors to consider the impact of changes in the economic climate on the business. For example, an entrepreneur that was expecting a recession to hit in the near future might be wary of investing in a venture that had a high break-even level of sales. On the other hand, businesses operating on a low cost basis may be an attractive prospect in such a scenario – their margin of safety would potentially be higher.

Break-even charts and analysis therefore provide a useful tool for entrepreneurs, investors and banks to make a judgement about the viability of a business and its chances of success. A series of 'what if' scenarios can be tested and this can help with business planning and the management of risk – a key area of focus for start-ups and established businesses alike.

It is worth noting, however, that the assumptions used to carry out the analysis are often based on variables that are notoriously hard to predict, such as the performance of the economy and consumer behaviour. Therefore, a degree of caution is advisable when projections of costs, revenues and profits are used to justify an investment decision.

Exam style question 3

1. Which two of the following are examples of fixed costs? *(2 marks)*
   (a) Annual licensing fee paid by a London taxi driver.
   (b) The napkins given out to customers by a sandwich shop.
   (c) The steel used in a car plant.
   (d) Restaurant staff employed on zero hours contracts.
   (e) Salary paid to the manager of a retail outlet.
2. Explain one advantage for an entrepreneur that performs break even analysis as part of their business planning. *(3 marks)*
3. Explain one limitation of break-even analysis. *(3 marks)*
4. Discuss whether a business should proceed with a new venture if the margin of safety is projected to be low. *(6 marks)*

Key terms

Break-even analysis is a management tool used to identify the output level where sales revenues equal total costs.

Costs are items of expenditure incurred by a business, e.g. wages, salaries, rent, fuel bills, advertising expenses and accountancy fees.

Fixed costs are costs that have to be paid regardless of how much a business produces or sells, e.g. salaries and rent.

Interest is the reward for saving or the cost of borrowing. It is usually calculated as a % of the original amount saved or borrowed.

Margin of safety is the numerical difference between a firm's level of sales and its break-even quantity. The larger the margin of safety, the better it is for the business.

Revenue is the money coming into a business from the sale of goods and/or services.

Total costs are the sum of all fixed costs and all variable costs.

Variable costs are costs that change as the level of output increases, e.g. raw material costs and payment of wages.

Chapter 1.3.3

Cash and cash flow

Aims

By the end of this chapter students should be able to understand:

- the importance of cash to a business.
- how to calculate and interpret cash-flow forecasts.

Cash

Businesses need to manage their day-to-day cash flow. The history books are littered with examples of businesses that failed not because their product was poor but because they simply ran out of cash. If a business cannot **pay its suppliers** then they will eventually stop supplying the stock, the gas will be disconnected and the landlord might take back control of the business premises. **Employees** will quickly grow impatient with being paid erratically or not being paid at all and will seek alternative employment. In short, without cash a business will have to stop trading almost immediately and the business will fail (become insolvent). Hence, cash is important to pay **suppliers**, **overheads** and **employees**.

The difference between cash and profit

Having the appropriate amount of cash is vital in order to stay solvent and compete in a market but it's important to note that while discounting stock excessively could solve a cash flow problem it may generate a new issue – lack of profits! In addition, generating cash flow through offering large discounts can signal that a business is in distress and harm a customer's confidence in their ability to provide a good service over the long term. Profit is the difference between sales revenue and total costs and expenses of a business (see Chapter 1.3.2). Profits are calculated over a period of time. Cash is the amount of money held by a business (either in hand or at the bank) at a particular point in time. It is generated through sales of goods or assets. Cash in required to pay for the expenses incurred by the business.

Cash flow forecasting

Cash flow forecasting refers to the prediction of cash coming in and moving out of a business over a given period of time, e.g. the next 6 or 12 months. Being able to predict how cash will flow in and out of the business can help its financial management and decision-making.

Cash inflows are the receipts of a business whereas **cash outflows** are the outgoings (or payments). Cash outflows will include expenditure on items such as set-up costs, rent and the purchase of stock. Cash inflow comes mainly from sales revenues but can include sources such as government grants and bank loans. The difference between a firm's cash inflow and cash outflow at any point in time is called the **net cash flow**.

The **opening balance** is the amount of cash the business has at the start of the period and the **closing balance** is the cash balance at the end of the period once the net cash flow has been taken into account.

Net cash flow = Cash inflow – Cash outflow

The importance of cash flow forecasts

- As a major component of a business plan, the cash flow forecast can help a business to obtain finance from a bank or a private investor.
- It helps to ensure that a business allocates funds to make payments to suppliers, employees (wages and salaries), the government (taxes) and financial lenders (loan repayments).

- Essentially, cash flow forecasting helps managers to run their businesses more effectively; poor cash flow management will get businesses into a **liquidity problem** (when a business cannot repay its debts due to a lack of cash), with the threat of bankruptcy.

Cash flow forecasting formulae

Net cash flow	=	Cash inflow – Cash outflow
Closing balance	=	Opening balance + Net cash flow
Opening balance	=	Closing balance in preceding month

Causes of cash flow problems

- Sales are lower than expected.
- Costs are higher than budgeted.
- There are unexpected costs.
- Customers who buy on credit are slow to pay.

To solve cash flow problems, a business can increase its cash inflow. For example, it could strive to improve its marketing (to boost sales) or use a bank overdraft (see Chapter 1.3.4). Alternatively, the business could reduce cash outflows. For example, it could seek to improve trade credit with its suppliers or lease rather than buy equipment.

Exam style question

(a) Complete the 2-month cash flow forecast for Müller & Co.: *(2 marks)*

	January (£)	**February (£)**
Opening balance	0	
Sales revenue	1,200	800
Bank overdraft	0	0
Cash inflow	1,200	800
Wages	500	500
Electricity	200	200
Telecommunications	150	150
Advertising	100	150
Cash outflow	950	1000
Net cash flow	+250	
Closing balance	250	50

(b) Explain two causes of cash flow problems. *(4 marks)*

(c) Explain how a business can resolve its cash flow problems. *(4 marks)*

Chapter review questions

1. Why do all businesses need cash?
2. Explain the difference between cash and profit.
3. What is meant by 'cash flow forecasting'?
4. How is 'net cash flow' calculated?
5. What is a liquidity problem?
6. How is a firm's closing balance calculated?

Cash flow forecasting is a decision-making tool used to predict the cash flowing in and out of a business over a given period of time.

Key terms

Cash flow forecasting is a decision-making tool used to predict the cash flowing in and out of a business over a given period of time.

Cash inflows refer to the money coming into a business from sales and other sources such as government grants and bank loans.

Cash outflows are the outgoings of the businesses, such as payment of wages, raw materials and utility bills (gas, water and electricity bills).

Closing balance refers to the amount of cash flow at the end of a trading period, usually one month. This figure then becomes the 'opening balance' in the following time period.

Insolvency occurs when a business can no longer pay its debts and bills and the business fails.

Liquidity occurs when a business has liquidity when it has cash or assets which can be turned into cash and can therefore pay its bills.

Net cash flow is the money available for the daily running of a business. It is calculated by working out cash inflow minus cash outflow.

Opening balance refers to the cash balance at the beginning of a trading period (usually each month). It is equal to the value of the closing balance in the preceding time period (the previous month).

Solvent – a business is solvent when it has sufficient cash to repay its bills.

Chapter 1.3.4

Sources of business finance

Aims

At the end of this chapter, students should be able to understand:

The various sources of finance for a start-up or established small business:

- short-term sources.
- long-term sources.

Short-term sources of finance

A new business start-up is likely to face a lot of expenditure before it starts trading. Deposits need to be put down on premises, stationery needs to be purchased, supplies of stock and, perhaps, raw materials will need to be brought in before production can begin. An entrepreneur may need to identify an appropriate source of short term finance to cover costs such as these until revenue becomes available.

- A 30 day credit period is usually given as standard but an **extended period of trade credit from suppliers** can provide a business with liquidity and breathing space in the short term while it attempts to bring in more revenue to cover its liabilities. These will normally be offered interest free but it can be difficult for a start up to convince a supplier that they are creditworthy.
- An **overdraft** allows a business to withdraw more money than they have in their bank account until they are overdrawn to an agreed limit. Overdrafts can, however, be costly if businesses use them regularly. Interest rates are often high and eligibility for this line of credit will depend on the bank's evaluation of the risk of a default (where the business cannot pay back the borrowed sum).

Long-term sources of finance

Most businesses will have to, at times, pay for significant capital expenditure. Where a large investment is required it will usually make sense to pay for it over a longer period. This allows the payments to be spread in order to prevent an unmanageable stress on the finances which could threaten their survival.

- **Personal savings of owners** might be an option. This may be an appropriate source of finance if there is not a large amount of finance required and the owners have the money available in savings.
- **Venture capital** can be an effective way for businesses to generate long term investment. A venture capitalist can be a high net worth individual who is looking to take an equity stake in a business that seems to have growth potential. Rewards can be high for venture capitalists but investments such as these are risky and so the business receiving the investment may have to give up a very high proportion of the business in return.
- **Share capital** can be used by limited companies to finance growth and investment. Finding investors willing to take shares in the business is not always easy; but families, friends or even employees are often willing to become shareholders. However, shareholders will want dividends which would mean reduced profit for the existing owners. It is worth noting that the owners will sacrifice some of their own equity when they finance the business this way but this can be an acceptable consequence provided the business grows more profitable as a result.
- **Bank loans** are issued to firms at every stage of their development but start-ups may find them harder to secure due to the heightened risk profile. Loans offer a predictable repayment schedule and a fixed payment that can give the owners certainty. However, the repayments can be a strain on the cash flow of a business that is yet to establish itself in a market and the interest rate might be high if the risk of default is perceived by the bank to be significant.

- **Retained profit** is profit that is not distributed to shareholders in the form of dividends and is held back for reinvestment instead. This is a useful source of finance for a firm as it does not need to be repaid like a loan and will not require giving up any equity in the business in order to access. Companies such as Apple use this type of financing for their enormous research and development investment. However, new firms will obviously not have the opportunity to use this source of funds.
- **Crowdfunding** is the practice of financing a venture via raising funds from a large number of contributors. It has harnessed the power of social media to spread the message of a business idea to potential investors who may have an affinity for the product or service or a personal link to the budding entrepreneur. It is common practice to offer donors 'free' goods or services once the business has started trading as a thank you for the contribution, rather than giving away equity.

All of the choices that a business can make will have their potential advantages and drawbacks. These factors are summarised in Figure 1.3.4a on page 34. The right choice of finance will depend on the particular circumstances the business finds itself in.

Factors affecting the choice of finance

When deciding which sources of finance to use, a business might wish to consider the following questions:

- **What is the capital for?** If the finance is required for stock by a business that faces tight cash flow, then an extended period of trade credit might be the best option. If the finance is needed to buy land then a long term bank loan secured against the property called a **mortgage** might make sense.
- **How much does the company need to raise?** If it is a relatively small amount then retained profit might cover it. However, if an extremely large sum is needed then a combination of different external methods might be needed. For example, when Tottenham Hotspur FC in the English Premier League needed to raise money to build their new stadium in 2017 they secured loan finance from investment banks and sold the naming rights.
- **What is the cost of the preferred method?** If a business has an option to extend trade credit terms with a supplier rather than use a bank overdraft, they will save on interest and reduce costs. This is a key consideration for most firms when seeking finance.
- **What is the existing debt level of the business?** If a business has taken on too much debt then interest payments will increase costs, reduce profits and become a drain on cash flow. A business with high debt levels might wish to seek alternatives to adding more debt.

Crowdfunding is the practice of financing a venture via raising funds from a large number of contributors.

Figure 1.3.4a

Choice of finance	Advantages	Disadvantages
Personal savings	• No interest payable. • Can be organised quickly if needed in an emergency.	• Owners may not wish to invest more capital in the business. • Owners may not have the assets or they may be tied up in illiquid assets such as property.
Retained profit	• No interest payable.	• Business profit earnings may be insufficient. • Reduces dividend payable to shareholders if a Ltd or PLC.
Sale of surplus assets/share capital	• Assets which are not contributing to the health of the company may now be put to use.	• Assets such as capital might be needed should output levels expand in future. • Business may not get a good price if a quick sale is needed. • Assets may be obsolete and impossible to sell.
Extended trade credit	• Cheap way to finance purchases of stock or to ease liquidity problems.	• Suppliers may refuse. • Relationships with suppliers may be strained.
Reduction of stock	• Stock may be tying up overly large amounts of cash. • If the product is highly liquid then finance can be raised easily.	• Stock is sold off cheaply which reduces the profitability of the business. • Selling off too cheaply could damage the brand.
Bank loans	• Banks are usually receptive to applications from soundly run businesses. • A fixed repayment each month can easily be built in to budgets and cash flow planning.	• Interest repayments can harm the cash flow position of the business.
Overdraft	• Usually quick and easy to arrange. • Allows flexibility – cash is there if and when needed and can be paid back flexibly.	• Interest rates are usually higher than those charged on bank loans.
Sale of shares	• Allows large amounts of money to be raised for effective and large expansion. • No interest payable or repayment schedule.	• Owners lose a percentage of profits through payment of dividends. • The existing owners can lose control of the business if they don't keep a majority stake.
Grants	• Free money (no need to repay).	• Very competitive to apply for. • Conditions are often attached. • Application is a lengthy process so they cannot remedy an emergency financial problem.
Venture capital	• Money loaned to the business in return for a share of the business. The business may be high risk due to being a business new to the market.	• Business has to give away potentially a high percentage of the business which leads to a loss of share capital and therefore loss of complete control of the business.
Loans from family/friends	• Low interest payable. • 'Softer' terms and conditions.	• Not all businesses will have this option. • Can damage personal relationships if the business cannot meet its commitments.
Crowd funding	• Funds can be raised easily from donations paid via social media and the internet and often the money is donated and does not have to be repaid.	• Insufficient funds may be raised. The business may have to buy gifts or extend privileges to people who invested in the business.

Exam style question

AG Silver PLC is a silver mining company. It is listed on the London Stock Exchange. The company has recently made a large profit on a mine in Mexico but the silver is now exhausted. It is considering further exploration in South America to find more silver deposits.

AG has worked out that the exploration project will cost £1.3m. It has been offered loan finance for the project from a bank that will cost £11,850 per month over 10 years.

Calculate the total interest AG will pay for this loan as a percentage of the amount borrowed.

(2 marks)

Chapter review questions

1. Explain the difference between internal and external finance.
2. Why might a sale of assets not be a very good idea for a capital intensive business?
3. Why is the sale of shares considered as a long term source of finance?
4. Why are overdrafts best only in the short term?
5. What are the disadvantages of asking for improved credit terms?
6. Why might a business prefer to take out a loan rather than reinvest profits?
7. Why might a partnership be reluctant to become a 'Ltd' company in order to sell shares to raise finance?
8. Why might a loan from family or friends not be preferable to borrowing from a bank?
9. What might be the most effective source of finance for a business with a high level of borrowing?
10. Why is selling stock inventory only a short term method of finance?

Key terms

External finance is finance that a business generates from individuals, businesses and organisations that it does not ordinarily trade with.

Finance is money that a business needs in order to operate and invest for the future.

Internal finance is money that a business can generate through its own trading.

Long term finance is finance required by businesses over a timeframe exceeding one year. It is usually used for investment expenditure.

Short term finance is finance that is required by businesses over the short run, i.e. less than one year. This is usually needed to solve short-term liquidity (cash flow) problems.

Chapter 1.4.1

The options for start-up and small businesses

Aims

By the end of this chapter, students should be able to understand:

- the concept of limited liability and unlimited lability.
- the implications for the business owner(s) of limited and unlimited liability.
- the types of business ownership for start-ups: sole trader, partnership, and private limited company.
- the advantages and disadvantages of each type of business ownership.
- the option of starting up and running a franchise operation.
- the advantages and disadvantages of franchising.

© Edexcel, 2017

The legal forms of business organisation

This chapter introduces the main types of legal forms of businesses for start-ups and small businesses in the UK. They can be classified as: sole traders, partnerships, limited liability companies, and franchises. Each has its own merits and drawbacks, which help the owners to determine the best type of legal form for their business organisation.

A business owner(s) has two main choices: to set up a business with limited or unlimited liability.

Limited liability and unlimited liability

Limited liability means that there is a legal difference between the owners of a company and the business itself. Limited liability protects shareholders who, in the event of the company going bankrupt, will lose no more than they invested in the company, i.e. they cannot be forced to sell their personal possessions to repay the debts of the company. In legal terms, there is a **divorce of ownership and control** since the owners (shareholders) are treated as separate legal entities from those who control and run the business (the directors and managers). A limited company can be sued and also sue in its own right.

Unlimited liability occurs when the business owner is not separate from the business which is the case for sole traders and partnerships (see explanations later in this Chapter). The debts of the business are the owners' responsibility. This means that if the business goes into debt and makes a loss, the owner is personally liable for repaying the debts, even if this means personal assets have to be sold to do so. This is because there is no legal difference between the owner (sole trader or partner) and the business (sole proprietorship or partnership). The business owner will be personally liable for any damages caused by their business.

The types of business ownership for start-ups: Sole traders

A **sole trader** is a business owned by a single person (known as the **sole trader**). This person can employ as many people as needed, but remains the only owner of the business. The advantages of being a sole trader include being able to:

- Set up the business easily. This is because sole proprietorships are the cheapest and easiest type of business to set up – there are very few legal procedures needed to start the business.
- Have autonomy (independence) in decision-making, i.e. the owner is the boss and does not need to consult anyone about his or her decisions. This makes the business relatively easy to run.
- Keep all the profits made by the business. This also gives an incentive for the sole trader to work hard as s/he is rewarded (see Chapter 1.1.2) with more profits as the business becomes more successful.
- Enjoy tax advantages as a small business.

- Ensure privacy as the business does not need to publish its accounts to the general public. Only the tax authorities need to see the financial information of the sole trader.
- Be flexible in what the business does. For example, the owner has some flexibility in the choice of working hours. Also, if one business idea does not work out, the sole trader can quite easily introduce new trading activities or close down the business and start another one.
- Have a sense of achievement from running their own business.

The disadvantages of being a sole trader include:

- The owner bears all the risks of running the business on his/her own. There is no one else to share the burden or responsibilities.
- The added workload from having to run the business as a sole proprietor. As the only person in the business, the sole trader often has to work long hours (especially during the early stages of the business being set up).
- Limited specialisation – Unlike large companies, sole traders cannot rely on the marketing, finance, production and human resource management expertise of others. This limits the extent to which sole proprietors can benefit from specialisation and the division of labour.
- Access to a variety of sources of finance (see Chapter 1.3.4) is limited. Being a small business, the sole proprietorship represents high risk. This limits the extent to which the sole trader can raise finance from banks and other sources.
- The lack of continuity – if the owner is sick or wishes to go on holiday, then the organisation will struggle to continue. If the owner dies, the business will cease to operate in its current legal form.
- Restricted ability to exploit economies of scale – large businesses are usually able to enjoy **economies of scale**, i.e. lower unit costs of production resulting from large scale operations. This means that sole traders struggle to gain cost advantages and therefore have to charge higher prices for their products.
- The owner has unlimited liability.

The types of business ownership for start-ups: Partnerships

A **partnership** is a business organisation owned by more than one person. In an **ordinary partnership**, there are between 2 and 20 owners, known as **partners** (the co-owners of the partnership). At least one of these partners will have unlimited liability, although it is usual practice for all the partners to share responsibility for any losses made by the business. The government does allow some businesses, such as law firms and health clinics, to operate with more than 20 partners.

To prevent potential misunderstandings and conflict, most partnerships draw up a legal contract between the partners, known as a **deed of partnership**. The contents of the partnership deed include the names of all partners, the amount of capital invested by each partner (and hence their stake in the partnership), their responsibilities, voting rights, arrangements for dismissing a partner or approving a new partner, and how profits are to be shared between the owners. If a deed of partnership is not prepared, then The Partnership Act of 1890 applies, stating that legally all partners have an equal share in the running of the business and the distribution of its profits.

The advantages of partnerships include:

- As there are up to twenty owners, a partnership is usually able to raise far more capital to run its business than sole traders.
- Similarly, as there are more owners, the business can benefit from having more ideas and expertise. Most partnerships can also benefit from specialisation and division of labour.
- Like sole traders, the business affairs of partnerships are kept confidential. Again, only the tax authorities need to know about the financial position of the business. This makes it appropriate for businesses such as private health care providers, accountancy firms and law firms to operate as partnerships as they need to keep their business affairs confidential.

- As partnerships tend to be small businesses, there tends to be good working relationships with both colleagues and customers. One of the potential drawbacks of being a large organisation is the lack of clear communication between staff, because there are simply too many of them.
- Unlike sole traders, there is improved continuity as the partnership can remain in business if a partner is ill or goes on holiday.
- In some cases, additional finance can be raised from **silent partners** (also known as **sleeping partners**). These partners simply invest in the business without taking an active role in the running of it.

The disadvantages of partnerships include:

- As there is more than one owner, there might be disagreements and conflict between the partners. This can undoubtedly harm the running of the partnership.
- Although the business can operate on a larger scale compared to sole traders, any profits made must be shared between all the owners.
- In most cases, the partners have unlimited liability. Although it is possible to have limited liability partnerships, this usually applies to sleeping partners only as they are not directly involved in the day to day running of the partnership so are not personally liable for any debts incurred.

In partnerships there might be disagreements and conflict between the partners.

The types of business ownership for start-ups: Private limited company

All private limited liability companies in the UK must be registered with the Registrar of Companies, a government agency that keeps records of all limited liability companies in the country. To set up a limited liability company, the owners must submit two important documents:

- **The Memorandum of Association** – a relatively short document that records the name of the limited company, its registered business address, the amount of share capital and an outline of the company's operations (what it does).
- **The Articles of Association** – a relatively longer document that contains information about:
  - The details and duties of the directors of the company.
  - Shareholders' voting rights.
  - The transferability of shares.
  - Details and procedures for the Annual General Meeting.
  - How profits are to be distributed (dividend policy).
  - Procedures for winding up (closing) the company.

Once the Registrar of Companies is satisfied with the paperwork, a **Certificate of Incorporation** is issued to the limited company so that it can start trading. The shareholders elect a **Board of Directors** (BOD) to represent their interests. The BOD is in charge of the strategic management of the company on behalf of its shareholders. The top director on the BOD is known as the **Managing Director** (MD) who oversees the operations of the company. It is at the Annual General Meeting that shareholders vote in the BOD to represent their interests.

Table 1.4.1a: Characteristics of a private limited company

	Private Limited Company
Legal status	Carries the initials 'Ltd.' after its name in official business communication.
Buying shares	Shares are not available on an open stock exchange, thereby limiting the amount of funds.
Selling shares	Shares can only be sold to family, friends and employees with the prior approval of the majority of the shareholders. This can make it difficult to sell shares in the company.
Start-up share capital	£2
Number of shareholders	No upper limit.
Raising further finance	The sale of more shares in the company must be first approved by the directors.

The advantages of limited companies include:

- Shareholders have limited liability.
- Additional finance can be raised through selling shares.

The disadvantages of limited companies include:

- Companies have to file their financial accounts and have these audited (checked) by an accountant. Various other documents also have to be sent to the Registrar of Companies at Companies House. This is both time consuming and potentially expensive.
- Companies are more administratively difficult, time consuming and expensive to set up compared to sole proprietorships and partnerships.

The option of starting up and running a franchise operation

Some organisations, known as **franchisors**, sell the right to other businesses to use their company name, logo, slogans and trademarks. Examples of franchises include McDonald's, Costa Coffee and Subway. The purchasing business is known as the **franchisee**. In return for the use of the franchise, the franchisee has to pay a certain percentage of its sales revenue (known as a **royalty payment**) to the franchisor.

The major advantage of franchises is their low failure rate. According to a recent CNN report, the failure rate of Subway and Dunkin Donuts are only 7% and 8% respectively. This is largely because of the interrelated benefits to both franchisor and franchisee (see Table 1.4.1b). Once established, a business development manager provides ongoing support and advice to the franchisee.

Table 1.4.1b

Advantages to franchisor	**Advantages to franchisee**
The franchisee will be suitably selected and will be determined to succeed.	The franchise business model has already been tried and tested, proving to be successful.
The franchisee has to pay a large sum of money to buy the franchise rights. This allows the franchisor to expand at a fast rate at a relatively low cost.	Costs can be significantly lower than starting a new business, as market research and promotions are done by the franchisor.
The franchisor does not have to get involved in hiring store managers or overseeing the running of the business.	The franchisor provides ongoing support, such as continuing training, sales promotion, insurance cover and budgeting and tax advice.

(continued overleaf)

Disadvantages to franchisor	Disadvantages to franchisee
The selection and training process of a suitable franchisee is quite long (over 1 year for a McDonald's franchise in the UK).	The costs – franchisees need to purchase the business and to pay annual royalty payments (a proportion of the sales revenue) to the franchisor.
Some franchisees run their business quite poorly, delivering sub-standard service.	Despite owning the business, there is less flexibility and freedom as the franchise agreement requires the franchisee to operate in a certain way.
The reputation of the business is no longer in the direct control of the franchisor.	The business cannot be sold without the prior agreement of the franchisor.

Exam style questions

1. Identify two features of partnership. *(2 marks)*
2. Explain one advantage to an owner of a private limited company of having limited liability. *(3 marks)*
3. Analyse the decision of a person wishing to start up a business by buying a franchise. *(6 marks)*

Chapter review questions

1. Explain the meaning of unlimited liability.
2. Explain the meaning of limited liability.
3. What are the four main legal forms of business organisation in the UK for start-ups and small businesses?
4. What are the key advantages and disadvantages of a sole proprietorship?
5. Outline the details that might appear in a 'deed of partnership'.
6. What is the difference between a franchisee and a franchisor?
7. What are the advantages and disadvantages of franchising as a form of business organisation?

Key terms

Franchises are a form of business organisation that has permission to use the name, logo and business model of another organisation. Examples include McDonald's, Starbucks and 7-Eleven.

Limited liability means that there is a legal difference between the owners of a company and the business itself, so there is a limit to the liabilities of the owner.

Partnerships are owned by between two to twenty owners (known as 'partners'). They pool funds and take risks together, but have to share profits between all owners.

Private limited company is a business organisation in which the owners and the business have separate legal identities and the owners' liability is limited to the amount they have put into the business.

Sole trader is a person who owns and runs a business as single proprietor. S/he takes all the risks but keeps any profit made by the business.

Unlimited liability occurs when the business owner is not separate from the business which is the case for sole traders and partnerships.

Chapter 1.4.2

Business location

Aims

By the end of this chapter, students should be able to understand:

Factors influencing business location:

- proximity to: market, labour, materials and competitors.
- nature of the business activity.
- the impact of the internet on location decisions.

The location decision

Why is London such a popular location option for businesses that operate in the financial services space? Why are there so many tech companies based near Edinburgh? Why are so many of the world's customer service call centres located in India? When businesses decide where to locate all or part of their business operations the decision is critical for the business. The right location choice can aid all aspects of the business from production and logistics to human resource management whilst the wrong decision can lead to business failure.

When a firm considers where to locate there are many factors that might be considered, and the factors that have most influence on the decision will vary according to the nature of different businesses. For example, service-based industries are likely to have different priorities to firms operating in product markets. Similarly, large firms might have a greater range of options than small firms operating in local markets.

Factors affecting the location decision

- **Proximity to the market** – The South East of England has some of the most expensive real estate in the world whilst in parts of the North of England, Wales and Scotland rents and land prices are much cheaper. A business looking to establish itself in the UK might save a very large amount of money by choosing a provincial town but London may still be preferred if the market in which it is operating is based there.
- **Proximity to labour** – When the Japanese car maker Nissan was looking for a European manufacturing base they chose to locate in Sunderland, in the North East of England. The area had a significant amount of unemployment due to the declining coal industry, allowing their recruitment needs to be met easily. In addition, many of the practical skills needed would have been available due to the industrial character of the region.
- **Proximity to raw materials** – For example, a company that relies on a large amount of raw materials such as Findus, the seafood ready-meals manufacturer, would save a considerable amount of money on transport and logistics by locating the factory close to the source of the raw materials through choosing a coastal site.
- **Proximity to competitors** – For many firms, locating in an area where they have no significant competitors is desirable as they can enjoy a monopoly in that local market and any competitors would mean having to compete for market share. However, in some industries businesses need to locate in the same area as their competitors so that they are where their customers expect them to be and can monitor their competitors' operations more closely. In addition, it may be the case that most of the professionals that the business would hope to attract are already employed in the area and there is a network of ancillary suppliers to the sector already in place. Attempting to set up in another region would therefore potentially be more difficult and costlier.

When marketing a product as a premium item then the store location may need to reflect that to ensure the brand image is maintained in the eyes of the consumer.

Nature of the business activity

- **Branding** – If you are marketing your product as a premium item then the location may need to reflect that to ensure the brand image is maintained in the eyes of the consumer. High-end car showrooms or purveyors of expensive furniture may choose to locate themselves in Chelsea or a similarly exclusive district of London for this reason.
- **Visibility** – The requirement to have a visible shop front is also an important factor. Car repair services are often found in back streets or in railway arches because they usually rely on referrals to generate business rather than the 'footfall' required by a retailer who might be best placed on the High Street (town centre).
- **The importance of transport and communications infrastructure** – A business with a large export division may wish to locate close to a sea or airport. A business which sells products to a nationwide market in a large country will benefit from being close to good road or rail links. A software company like Google would need to locate in a country with excellent ICT infrastructure.
- **Government inducements** – certain types of business are sometimes offered subsidies and incentives to locate in certain areas as part of a wider industrial strategy. This can be very attractive for a start-up company lacking capital.

The impact of the internet on location decisions: e-commerce and/or fixed premises

The internet is an ever-growing market place. Online shopping has completely changed the way in which consumers shop and while it has meant new opportunities for some businesses it has brought extremely challenging conditions for many established retailers.

E-commerce (see Chapters 1.4.3 & 1.5.2) has enabled smaller businesses to access markets that would have seemed impenetrable before due to large set up costs and the need for a retail premises. It has allowed businesses to market their goods more easily and reach consumers in parts of the country that might have been previously off limits. Many businesses are, therefore, scaling down their High Street operations and moving more of their trade to the online space where costs are lower and the potential market is larger.

However, a physical retail environment (**fixed premises**) with knowledgeable sales staff on hand can help to sell the product and so there are many businesses for whom a fixed premises is vital. For example, many would not spend a large sum on a car without taking it for a test drive and the ambience created in store can be a key part of the brand and can communicate an impression of quality to the consumer.

It is also important to note that consumers do not always wish to opt for the convenience of shopping online. For many, a visit to a mall or Retail Park is an experience that they enjoy and value. For example, a bridal wear shop will give appointments to bridal parties and provide them with a fun, focused and tailored service that might not easily be replicated online.

Exam style question 1

Discuss what a small business owner should consider when deciding where to locate a small business. *(6 marks)*

Chapter review questions

1. Why can access to raw materials play a large part in a business' location decision?
2. Explain why retail businesses might regard proximity to market as the most important location factor.
3. What might the costs and benefits be of choosing to locate in an area that is economically depressed?
4. Explain why a business needs to consider local labour markets when deciding where to locate.
5. Explain the reasons why many similar firms often choose to locate in the same areas.
6. How have new business technologies impacted on the location decisions of businesses?

Key terms

E-commerce is business activity which takes place over the internet.

Fixed premises are a physical shop or office.

Government subsidy is a sum of money given to a business to reduce costs or increase production or act as an incentive to locate in a particular area of the country.

Infrastructure is the equipment and systems that exist in a country that provide a platform for business to be done such as roads, transport links and telecommunications.

Location is the site or sites that a business chooses to base its operations.

Chapter 1.4.3

The marketing mix

Aims

By the end of this chapter, students should be able to understand:

- what the marketing mix is and the importance of each element (price, product, promotion, and place).
- how the elements of the marketing mix work together.
- the need to balance the marketing mix based on the competitive environment.
- the impact of changing customer needs on the marketing mix.
- the impact of technology on the marketing mix (e-commerce and digital communication).

What is the marketing mix?

Marketing is the entire process of researching the market to identify customer needs and wants, designing and producing a product to satisfy desires, to finally selling a product or service to a customer. The process of marketing helps to retain existing customers and attract new ones and therefore it is a very important part of business operations. The **marketing mix** is made of four components:

- identifying needs and wants of customers (market research – see Chapter 1.2.2).
- designing and producing a **product** which satisfies customer needs in a profitable way for the business.
- charging the correct **price** to customers.
- using the correct method of **promotion** to inform customers about the product.
- selecting an appropriate **place** to distribute and sell the product.

Every good or service has a marketing mix designed to encourage people to buy the product. A business will decide what to produce and who to produce it for. Such decisions will influence the price, method of promotion and where the product will be sold.

How the elements of the marketing mix work together

Many businesses operate in a competitive environment where there are many other businesses selling similar goods and services. Examples include: food takeaways, clothing shops, bakeries, cafés, hairdressers and recruitment agencies. To stand out from the competition, businesses need to differentiate themselves from rivals so they may choose to use all or some of the marketing mix.

Product

A unique selling point of a product is something which makes it different from their competitors. For example, a shop selling t-shirts may differentiate itself from others by using materials which are biodegradable and made from bamboo. A bakery may only use organic ingredients.

Pricing

A business may use promotional (discounted) pricing to attract customers to buy a particular type of product or to attract customers to their shop. A bakery may sell its products at half price after 6pm, which may attract customers at this time and offload perishable stock.

Promotion

A café or food takeaway may give customers a loyalty card who collect points or stamps which can be traded in for products or discounts when a certain number have accumulated. They may also have special offers or give discounts for bulk purchases, e.g. buy two items to get 20% discount, or buy three items to receive 40% discount.

Place

A bakery may have a website through which customers can order cakes for special occasions online, over the phone or in person. A café may allow customers to text or email in an order, make payment online and collect food and drink ordered at a designated time.

The impact of changing customer needs on the marketing mix

Product

A bakery may start to produce a line of bread and cakes which are gluten free to meet the increasing need for food catering to people on specialist diets. A sports shop may start to sell yoga mats and clothing in response to the increase in popularity of the pastime. There is an increasing trend for people to buy 'experiences' as gifts instead of traditional presents. For example, a ride in a hot air balloon, a drive in a classic car, or a series of cookery lessons.

Price

The increase in the popularity of smartphones has resulted in a decrease in price of smartphones due to mass production. For example, an Alcatel smartphone is priced at approximately £55. An increase in demand for short holiday breaks overseas has resulted in a decrease in the price of short haul flights caused by an increase in the number of budget airlines.

Promotion

Health and specialist food shops may email and send SMS messages to their customers to inform them of new products and the latest offers.

Place

Customers may buy products from a website or via an app. This has enhanced the convenience for customers who are able to purchase products online.

The impact of technology on the marketing mix

E-commerce and social media have changed the promotion and place aspects of the market mix as products can be purchased through websites and apps and social media has allowed communication between businesses and customers to be interactive and not just one way.

E-commerce influences how products are promoted and also how they get to the customer. Many businesses have a website through which customers can obtain information about the business and through which products are sold. Department stores, such as John Lewis, have physical stores and also sell online and as a consequence they can reach a much larger audience, which includes overseas customers, than if they only had physical stores. Online retailers such as eBay and Amazon reach a wide audience as customers are based around the world and people can shop 24/7. Buying through the internet has meant that customers have to provide e-retailers with their personal details and the business can subsequently track purchases and items they search for, which leads to personalised promotion of products via email a customer may be

Online retailers such as Amazon reach a wide audience as customers are based around the world and people can shop 24/7.

interested in. E-commerce has impacted how businesses get goods to consumers and how consumers can access goods. E-commerce has therefore changed the 'place' component of the marketing mix.

Firms communicate with customers and potential customers through social media platforms such as Instagram and Facebook. They may also communicate with customers by sending SMS messages and emails. Messages sometimes contain discount codes to encourage customers to purchase the goods or services; this is an example of promotion. Customers are encouraged to rate and provide feedback on products and services through social media and potential and future customers may research ratings to decide whether they will purchase the good or service. Vloggers (Video bloggers) often create videos about products which they upload to YouTube and are then shared on social media. Online reviews and ratings are an important source of information for consumers and have changed the way in which businesses communicate with their customers. Digital communication has changed the 'place' and 'promotion' components of the marketing mix.

Exam style questions

1. Analyse how digital communication has impacted the marketing mix of a restaurant. *(6 marks)*
2. Discuss ways in which a traditional bookshop can adapt their marketing mix in order to survive the competition posed by online booksellers such as www.bookdepository.co.uk and www.amazon.co.uk. *(12 marks)*

Chapter review questions

1. State the components of the marketing mix.
2. Explain how the competitive environment may impact the marketing mix of a fast food business.
3. Give an example of how changing customer needs may influence the marketing mix of a health food shop.
4. Give an example of how technology may impact the marketing mix of a sportswear manufacturer.
5. Discuss how e-commerce can assist small businesses.
6. Identify three methods of digital communication businesses can use to communicate with customers and potential customers.

Key terms

The **marketing mix** is the combination of marketing factors used by businesses to encourage consumers to buy their product, i.e. the 4 P's (product, price, promotion and place).

Place refers to the method or methods a business uses to get its product to the consumer.

Price refers to the amount paid by a customer to purchase a good or service.

Product is the aspect of the marketing mix that refers to developing and providing a product that consumers want to buy.

Promotion refers to the strategies a business can use to inform consumers about its products or services and persuade them to make a purchase.

Social media refers to digital communication platforms, such as Facebook, Instagram and Twitter.

Chapter 1.4.4

Business plans

Aims

By the end of this chapter, students should be able to understand:

- the role and importance of a business plan.
- the purpose of planning business activity.

The role and importance of a business plan

A **business plan** is created in the early stages of the life of a business, or a new business project. It is a document that describes an organisation's objectives and its strategies (plans) to achieve these goals. The contents of a business plan include the following information:

- the business idea (see Chapter 1.1.1).
- business aims and objectives (see Chapter 1.3.1).
- target market and market research (see Chapters 1.2.2 and 1.2.3).
- forecast revenue, cost and profit (see Chapter 1.3.2).
- cash-flow forecast (see Chapter 1.3.3).
- sources of finance (see Chapter 1.3.4).
- location (see Chapter 1.4.2).
- the marketing mix (see Chapter 1.4.3).
- the skills, qualifications and work experience of the business owners.

Business plans allow the owners to:

- Express their vision for the business in writing and therefore provide direction for owners and employees.
- Undertake market research to ensure that there is a market for the product or service and to work out the strength of competition.
- Find a suitable location for the business, as a poor location could mean few customers and an adverse impact on the cash-flow of the business (ultimately leading to business failure).
- Calculate how much finance will be needed to start the business or business venture.
- Work out the running costs and potential sales revenue.
- Design a suitable marketing mix for the business (see Chapter 1.4.3).

The purpose of planning business activity

The purposes of a well-written and researched business plan are to:

- Obtain finance to start the business.
- Identify risks and make plans to minimise risks of failure.

A good business plan will provide evidence of market research and financial planning to prove that the business has a realistic chance of success. Forecasts of sales help the business to plan how much stock to buy and whether it will be able to meet customer needs. Ultimately, a good business plan can help the organisation to improve its chances of success.

Obtaining finance

To obtain finance from a lender, a business must provide evidence that financial planning has taken place. Banks, business angels and venture capitalists (see Chapter 1.3.4) need realistic estimates of future costs and revenues (see Chapter 1.3.4) and cash-flow forecasts (see Chapter 1.3.3). They also need to be convinced that the idea for the business is going to work and therefore a good idea supported by evidence of thorough market research and identification of a target market are essential. Evidence of research into the location of the business is also required. Lenders are also interested in the skills, qualifications and work experience of the business owners as they need to be convinced that they have the background and experience to make the business a success. Lenders wish to know how a business will operate and if the business will be able to repay loans.

Minimising risk

Risk refers to any business situation that involves exposure to danger or financial loss. Careful planning and consideration of what could go wrong and negatively impact the business is required in order to minimise business risks. In addition, business needs to plan for how it would deal with any anticipated difficulties. Minimising risks are important for business survival.

According to www.smallbusiness.co.uk, approximately 60% of small businesses fail within the first 5 years of trading. The most common cause of business failure is cash-flow problems and therefore planning for situations when customers do not pay on time for goods and services and creation of strategies for the business to cope with cash-flow problems is essential for survival.

Clearly stated aims and objectives (see Chapter 1.3.1) for the business provide focus and direction for directors and workers, which will also contribute to the success of the business.

Exam style question 1

Cheryl and Thomas are Food Technology teachers who have decided to have a career change and start a cooking school. They have conducted market research and identified a target market of people who are interested in learning how to cook different cuisines and may purchase cooking courses as gifts for friends. Cheryl and Thomas need to ask the bank for a loan to renovate the premises, purchase kitchen equipment and set up a website. They approach you for advice about what they need to include in a business plan to aid their loan application.

Questions

1. Identify 2 examples of non-financial information that should be included in a business plan. *(2 marks)*
2. Identify 3 examples of financial information that must be included in the business plan. *(3 marks)*
3. Explain two reasons, in addition to the loan application, why Cheryl and Thomas need to produce a business plan. *(4 marks)*

Chapter review questions

1. List the various components of a business plan.
2. Why are aims and objectives an important part of a business plan?
3. Why is market research an essential part of a business plan?
4. Why is it important to research the location of a business?
5. What is the most common reason for business failure?
6. What financial information does a potential lender need to see?
7. Why is it important to plan for business risks?

Key terms

A **business plan** is a written document that describes an organisation's objectives and its strategies or plans to achieve these goals.

Capital describes the manufactured resources needed in a business e.g. machinery, tools, equipment, computers.

Risk refers to any business situation that involves exposure to danger or financial loss.

Chapter 1.5.1

Business stakeholders

Aims

By the end of this chapter, students should be able to understand:

- who business stakeholders are and their different objectives.
- how stakeholders are affected by business activity.
- how stakeholders impact business activity.
- possible conflicts between stakeholder groups.

Business stakeholders and their different objectives

Stakeholders are affected by and may impact on business activity. A **stakeholder** is any person, group of people or organisation affected in any way by the operations of the business or has a direct interest in the well-being of a business. The stakeholders of a business all have different aims and objectives.

- **Shareholders** (owners) and **potential shareholders** are interested to see the profits being made by the business in order to gauge the level of dividends and future earning potential. They wish to know whether the business has potential for growth to decide whether their investment or future investment is profitable. Shareholders may put pressure on directors to increase profits for their own future gain.
- **Employees** are concerned with their terms and conditions at work and may be interested in whether the business runs on ethical principles. Some businesses provide their employees with training and equip them with skills that are transferable to other jobs and occupations, thereby increasing the overall level of skills in the economy. This might influence whether a potential employee wants to work for the business. Employees might also use the financial accounts of the business to examine the extent to which they can push for a pay rise. They will have a stronger case for doing so if the firm earns higher profits.
- **Customers** are concerned with whether they are getting value for money when they buy goods and services from the business. They may also be concerned about where the business gets its materials, for example, whether damage is caused to the environment or whether workers or children are exploited in the production process. Some customers may be attracted by a business' fair trade policies and others may wish to pay the lowest piece possible. Customers are all business' source of sales revenue so it is very important for businesses to keep existing customers happy and to attract new customers.
- **Managers** are employees of the business and therefore have the same interests in the business as other employees. They may use the financial accounts to judge the success of the business and to set future targets. Managers also need to know who owes the business money (i.e. the debtors of the business) and who the business owes money to (i.e. the creditors of the business).
- **Suppliers** want to know whether they will get paid for the goods and services they sell on credit to other businesses. They are interested in whether the business can pay bills on time and its track record of repaying its debts. They may use financial information about the business to judge the extent to which it is likely to be able to repay its debts.
- The **local community** is interested in the operations of businesses as it may provide essential goods and services, provide jobs and training for employees and make a positive impact on the community. On the other hand, a business may cause noise and air pollution through its operations. There may be congestion around the business, caused by customers and also suppliers delivering goods or materials. A business may act ethically and respect its employees and the community in which it operates. For example, businesses work to educate young people and the general public, so therefore benefit society. Ethical businesses may also uphold principles of sustainable development and may ensure that their actions cause minimal negative impact on the environment. This may enhance the positive image of the business and boost sales and profits.

Some customers may choose not to go to Starbucks because they have caused local independent cafés or restaurants to close down in their local town.

- **Pressure groups** are groups of like-minded individuals who work together to put pressure on businesses and/or governments for change in business practices that benefit society as a whole. For example, Action on Smoking and Health (ASH) is a UK based anti-smoking pressure group that puts pressure on the government to introduce methods to reduce smoking.
- The **government** is also interested in the operations of a business as they provide jobs and contribute to the economic growth of the country. The government will also examine the financial statements of a business to ensure that it is paying the correct amount of tax.

How stakeholders may influence business

Customers may boycott shops which they consider act unethically or are against the interests of the local community. For example, some customers may choose not to go to Starbucks or McDonald's because they have caused local independent cafés or restaurants to close down in their local town. Businesses may lose environmentally conscious customers if they do not implement environmentally friendly initiatives like their competitors.

Examples of how pressure groups influence businesses may include:

- Preventing a business locating in an area of natural beauty.
- Preventing the building of a road through an already congested area.
- Preventing the location of a nightclub or bar in a residential area.
- Reducing the amount of air pollution caused by a business.
- Criticism in the media about actions of a business which negatively impacts the environment or endangers the health of the general public.

The government may influence the location of businesses by providing grants or tax breaks to encourage firms to locate in an area of high unemployment. It may provide subsidies to businesses to encourage production of certain goods and services, for example goods using solar energy, social enterprises or those businesses employing workers with individual special needs or the long term unemployed. Governments may also subsidise firms who train workers and provide them with skills which are transferable to other industries.

Possible conflicts between stakeholder groups

Every stakeholder group has its own interest in a business, but this may conflict with those of other stakeholder groups. Some examples of such conflict include:

Shareholders and employees
Shareholders may wish to maximise profits and their personal returns and therefore may be against pay rises for employees. Employees, on the other hand, may wish to maximise their income and petition management for better pay and working conditions.

Managers and shareholders
Managers may support shareholders with their desire for higher profits or may support workers because they know that better pay and working conditions will improve the morale and productivity of workers.

Management and local community
Managers may wish to maximise profits and therefore choose the cheapest method of production which may not be friendly for the environment or may indulge in practices which have a negative impact on the local community. For example, the local community may disapprove of the noise pollution caused by a restaurant or bar that opens until late and is located in a residential area.

Managers and customers
Managers aim to maximise profits and may choose to produce lower quality goods and provide a less than ideal service by employing fewer workers. However, customers want value for money and to buy quality goods and services at a reasonable price. They also expect a decent level of customer service. Hence, this can create conflict between different stakeholders.

Business and the environment
Some businesses may deliberately choose not to use environmentally friendly methods of production in order to cut costs, but this may damage the natural and ecological environment. Some businesses may use excessive packaging, which can create wastage and be a strain on scarce resources.

Businesses and suppliers
Suppliers wish to be paid as quickly as possible after delivering goods to the business. The business may wish to delay payment and extend the period of credit so that it can hold onto the cash for longer. Hence, there can be conflict between a business and its suppliers.

Exam style question 1

People Tree is a UK based clothing company that makes garments from materials sourced from 15 different countries. All materials are purchased on a fair trade basis. Any services, such as embroidery, stitching and weaving, are also paid for on a fair trade basis. This means that the prices of the garments are pitched at a level which covers production costs and allows the producers to make a profit instead of being based on the global market price for that material as this can often be less than the production costs. This arrangement makes it possible for profits to be fed back into the community. The methods of production are all designed to minimise the impact on the environment. For example, all its dyes are natural.

Source: adapted from www.peopletree.co.uk

(a) Identify and explain two ways in which People Tree has a positive impact on the community where the garments are made. *(6 marks)*

(b) Discuss how ethical principles can influence a business. *(9 marks)*

Exam style question 2

Patagonia is an outdoors clothing designer and retailer. They work to protect the global environment by using production techniques that aim to minimise the impact on the environment, by trying to reduce and recycle waste and use some of their profits to support charities and other non-profit making organisations that work to protect the environment.

(a) Analyse three ways in which care for the environment impacts upon the way Patagonia operates. *(6 marks)*

(b) Discuss the following statement, 'Patagonia makes a positive contribution to society'. *(9 marks)*

Chapter review questions

1. Explain the objectives of each of the following stakeholders of a business:
   (a) Shareholders
   (b) Employees
   (c) Customers
   (d) Managers
   (e) Suppliers
   (f) Local community
   (g) Pressure groups
   (h) The government
2. Give an example of a pressure group and explain how its actions impacted upon a business of your choice.
3. Explain how employees may influence the performance of a business.
4. Explain how shareholders may influence the actions of a business.
5. Explain the potential conflict which may arise between an employee and a manager.
6. Explain the potential conflict which may arise between a manager and a supplier to a business.

Key terms

Environmental issues are concerned with how production and consumption of goods and services affects the natural environment.

An **ethical** business is one which bases its decisions on underlying moral principles and values.

Fair trade is when producers are paid a price for their goods which covers the costs of production and allows the producers to make a profit, which may be reinvested into the local community.

A **grant** is a gift of money from the government or non-governmental organisation given to a business or individual for a particular purpose which does not have to be repaid.

Pressure groups are clusters of like-minded individuals who work together to put pressure on businesses and/or governments for change for the betterment of society.

Shareholders are the owners of a limited company (private limited or public limited company).

A **stakeholder** is any person, group of people or organisation which is affected in any way by the operations of the business or has a direct interest in its well-being.

Sustainable development refers to economic development which satisfies current needs but does not use up the earth's resources so that the needs of future generations are compromised.

A **tax break** is when a business is allowed to pay no tax or a lower rate of tax on profits for a limited period of time.

Chapter 1.5.2

Technology and business

Aims

By the end of this chapter, students should be able to understand:

- different types of technology used by businesses.
- how technology influences business activity.

Different types of technology

Businesses use different types of technology for many purposes, which include: selling, promotion, communicating with customers, collecting payment, ordering stock and in the production process. Different types of technology include the following:

E-commerce

Many businesses sell goods over the internet. This is known as **e-commerce** (see Chapter 2.2.4). Businesses such as Amazon act as online department stores. eBay allows people to buy and sell a huge range of goods on their website, and www.notonthehighstreet.co.uk is a selling platform for a large number of small businesses promoting and selling goods which may not be found in shopping malls and other popular shopping destinations.

E-commerce has changed the way in which some businesses operate. For example, Uber operates its taxi service through an app. Airbnb has a website through which people offer their homes for others to rent for short periods of time. Businesses can exist on the internet (e-business) and therefore do not need to rent retail premises, which reduces their costs. At the same time there has been a rise in the number of people shopping online or through mobile apps. For example, flights and holidays can be purchased online and for a growing number of people there is no need to visit a travel agent.

Social media

Many businesses use social media such as Instagram, Facebook, and Twitter to promote their products and services and to keep customers updated with new products and trends. Social media also acts as a means of communicating with customers. Some businesses may have their own Facebook page and Instagram account and actively encourage customers to post reviews, ratings of products and services and to ask questions. Businesses may post information on social media about new products, information about promotional events and photographs of customers and celebrities using their products.

LinkedIn is used by a growing number of businesses when trying to recruit new employees and when searching for potential customers. It is also a useful online tool for making contact with individuals who work in the same industry or profession or when trying to find somebody who can provide services to the business, such as web designers, graphic designers or accountants.

Musicians, actors, politicians, and journalists often use Twitter as a way of communicating with people and as a means of gaining publicity ('followers'). Businesses may tweet about famous people using their products and to keep customers informed about recent products and activities of the business.

LinkedIn is used by a growing number of businesses when trying to recruit new employees and when searching for potential customers.

Digital communication

Digital communication has changed the way in which businesses communicate with customers. For example:

- Use of email makes communication with staff and customers easier (see Chapter 1.4.3).
- Websites which review goods and services, such as Trip Advisor or Trust Pilot, are often used by individuals when deciding which good or service to purchase.
- Almost all businesses have a website which stakeholders (see Chapter 1.5.1) can use to access information about the business or its products.
- When a customer buys goods online, the business has access to their personal information and with permission can send customers personal emails about promotions and events.
- Purchasing patterns of customers can be tracked and used by businesses when customers create an online account with a business or sign up for its loyalty programmes. These include, for example, Tesco's Club Card and Sainsbury's Nectar card.
- QR code readers allow people to access websites, videos and other information by scanning a code on a poster or display. It provides a convenient and quick way for people to access information.
- Businesses can send SMS messages or text messages to customers. This is a personalised means of communication and businesses can inform customers about products and promotions which may interest them. They may ask customers to rate their product or service by responding to the SMS. This is an example of two-way communication.

Payment systems

Technology has broadened the ways in which customers can pay for their goods and services. For example, contactless debit and credit cards have speeded up the amount of time it takes to pay for a product as customers tap their credit card or debit card over a card reader which accepts payment up to a certain limit. PayPal provides businesses and customers with a secure means of accepting payment for goods purchased online and is especially beneficial to small businesses who do not wish to pay high costs for accepting payment by the major credit card companies. Apple Pay, Android Pay and Samsung Pay are systems which allow people to pay for goods and services using their smartphones. Some businesses offer discounts for customers using this method of payment because it reduces the high costs incurred when people pay by credit card, which is equal to approximately 2% of the value of goods or services purchased.

How technology influences business activity

Technology can influence business activity in terms of sales, costs and the marketing mix.

- **Sales** – E-commerce increases access to customers as businesses can sell to local and global markets. For example, a small shop in Dorset selling hand knitted jumpers can produce goods for shipment around the world. Customers are also able to shop 24 hours a day.
- **Costs** – E-commerce reduces the need for physical shops or as many physical shops as existed before the internet. This is because a business can become well-known even without having a physical presence. Delivery costs however increase, but this may be offset by reduced costs of retail space and higher sales.
- **Marketing mix** (see Chapter 1.4.3), which consists of the 4 Ps:
  - **Place** – E-commerce has changed the way many businesses get their goods to customers. Businesses may sell directly to customers (B2C) or to other businesses (B2B). For example, customers may buy clothing directly from Zara online. Groceries can be ordered from the supermarket and goods will be delivered to a customer's home.
  - **Product** – E-commerce has allowed customers to personalise the products they buy. For example, Moonpig is a popular website which allows customers to create greeting cards and personalised gifts online which are then sent to the person of their choice. The Nike website allows people to customise trainers and bags.

- **Promotion** – Businesses use their website, social media, and SMS messages to communicate with customers. Video advertisements may be shown on the television or in cinemas but most people will view them on YouTube on a smartphone or laptop computer. Videos are shared on social media and people often make their own video reviews of products and videos about how to use products and fix products. This is a form of free publicity for a business but of course the publicity may be positive and negative! Product and business ratings are very important to customers and businesses as endorsements by others is often attractive to customers. Many retailers offer online membership to customers who provide personal details and allow the business to collect information about spending habits and gather feedback via online questionnaires and ratings systems. They offer discounts, information about new products and exclusive offers in return for this valuable information, which ultimately helps them to respond better to customer needs and wants.
- **Price** – Promotional or discounted pricing may be offered to people who use discount codes which are often emailed to customers who have provided businesses with their personal information. For example, a supermarket may offer free delivery on orders over a certain amount. Businesses often send customers emails containing information about sales, or discounted goods.

Exam style question

Jonah manages a clothing shop called Saturday Night in a busy area of a town centre. His clothing range is aimed at young women and he stocks items in the shop and in a warehouse on the outskirts of town where rents are cheaper. Customers can buy clothes from the Saturday Night website and from the shop. Jonah has created a membership system and customers earn points for each purchase which can be traded in for free gifts, e.g. reusable bags with the Saturday Night logo and name. He has a Facebook page and also sends members an SMS message when new clothes have arrived in store.

Questions

1. Identify the ways in which Jonah has used technology in his business. *(3 marks)*
2. Analyse ways in which technology has impacted the marketing mix of Saturday Night. *(6 marks)*

Chapter review questions

1. Identify three examples of digital communication used by businesses to communicate with customers.
2. Explain two advantages of e-commerce.
3. Describe how e-commerce may impact sales of a business.
4. Explain how e-commerce may impact costs of a business.
5. Describe examples of how technology can impact the four components of the marketing mix: product, price, promotion and place.
6. Explain three ways technology may be an advantage to a business.
7. Explain three ways technology may be a disadvantage to a business.

Key terms

Digital communication refers to any communication of a digital nature, such as email, SMS messages, or Apps such as Snapchat, Instagram, and Twitter.

E-commerce is selling goods and completing business transactions over the internet.

Social media are communication platforms which are used to share content, ideas and facilitate collaboration, e.g. Facebook, Twitter, Instagram, and YouTube.

Chapter 1.5.3

Legislation and business

Aims

By the end of this chapter students should be able to understand:

- the purpose of legislation: the principles of consumer law and employment law.
- the impact of legislation on businesses.

Principles of consumer law: quality and consumer rights

Consumer legislation refers to the laws that have been passed by parliament to provide a minimum standard of customer care with regard to the quality of goods and protect shoppers from being misled or exploited. **The Consumer Rights Act 2015** incorporated the main principles of the Sales of Goods Act 1970 which are that goods should be:

1. **Of satisfactory quality** – this means that goods should not be faulty or damaged when purchased. The standard of quality that should be expected by a consumer is a subjective one. The goods should be of the quality a reasonable consumer would expect to receive given the amount paid.
2. **Fit for purpose** – this means that goods must perform the job that they were bought to carry out. For example, a raincoat that is not waterproof would fail this standard.
3. **As described** – this means that the goods must reasonably fit any description given. For example, a shoe described as having a full leather upper must indeed be made of leather and not have any plastic in its upper.

Any goods that do not adhere to this standard can be rejected by the consumer. The claim made is made against the seller and not the manufacturer of the goods. If the goods are rejected in the first 30 days then a full refund must be given. Once the 30 days are elapsed then, provided the claim is made within six months of purchase, goods sold in contravention of the standard must be either repaired or replaced according to the favoured option of the seller. A claim made beyond the six-month period is possible but the burden is on the consumer to prove that the fault existed at the time of purchase.

There is also provision for services within the act. Services should be:

1. Performed with reasonable care and skill
2. Any information given that is spoken or written is binding where the consumer relies on it.
3. Where the price is not agreed beforehand, the service must be provided for a reasonable price.
4. Unless a particular timescale for performing the service is set out or agreed, the service must be carried out in a reasonable time.

The provisions for redress that are given in the act if the criteria above are not met include the right to a repeat of the service or a right to a full or partial refund depending on the nature and quality of the service given.

Principles of employment law: recruitment

The Equality Act 2010 prevents a business from discriminating in favour of, or against, any person based on the following 'protected characteristics':

- age
- disability
- gender reassignment
- race
- religion or belief
- sex
- sexual orientation
- marriage and civil partnership
- pregnancy and maternity

This means that any company found to be discriminating in such a way can be taken to court and made to pay compensation to a claimant. The implications of this are significant for advertising for new recruits. To take the gender example, the advert cannot explicitly state that a particular gender is preferred and the language used in the advert or job description cannot imply that the job may be more suitable for a man or a woman.

At the shortlisting and interview stage businesses must not use selection criteria or ask questions that are discriminatory. For example, asking a woman whether she is planning to start a family is likely to be discrimination as a man would be very unlikely to have the same question asked of him.

Principles of employment law: pay

The Equality Act 2010 replaced the ground breaking **Equal Pay Act of 1970** which prohibited any less favourable treatment between men and women in terms of pay provided that the work done was broadly similar in nature and of equal value. Before the act was passed it was common for women to be paid at a lower rate than their male counterparts. It is still the case that a man doing the same role as a woman could be paid more due to a 'material factor' such as length of service or performance on the job, but this might have to be proven in a costly court case if the firm faces a legal challenge from a female claimant.

Principles of employment law: discrimination

If an individual feels that they have been denied employment, denied promotion opportunities or treated unfairly at work due to their having a 'protected characteristic' then they are entitled to make a complaint. If they are not satisfied with the outcome of the complaint then they are entitled to seek mediation where an outside body tries to bring the case to an acceptable resolution. If there is still no settlement then the party with the grievance can seek redress via a tribunal or in court.

Principles of employment law: health and safety

The Health and Safety at Work Act 1974 is the principal piece of legislation pertaining to occupational health and safety in the UK. It places a responsibility on businesses to "to ensure, so far as is reasonably practicable, the health, safety and welfare at work." The Act requires:

- safe operation and maintenance of the working environment, plant and systems.
- maintenance of safe access to the workplace.
- safe use, handling and storage of dangerous substances.
- adequate training of staff to ensure health and safety.
- adequate welfare provisions for staff at work.

There are many examples of how businesses have had to change their practices to stay within the provisions of the act such as: goggles and hard hats on building sites, nurses using gloves to treat patients and providing training to those that move heavy objects.

The impact of legislation on businesses: costs and consequences

Businesses will face **costs** in order to ensure compliance with all of the employment laws and directives that affect them. Human Resource departments are likely to be fastidious in their record keeping in order to ensure that they have stayed within the law in terms of their recruitment practices. Such administration takes time and costs money. Where tribunals and court cases are required then the legal costs can build up to the tens of thousands very easily.

Health and safety legislation will have implications for business costs. The personal protective equipment that they will be required to provide can be expensive. Claims made for compensation where accidents do happen can entail such a large liability as to be worth insuring against which is an expensive overhead in some industries. That said, gaining a reputation as an employer that does not take the safety of their employees seriously could be costlier still.

Exam style question

1. Identify which 2 of the following would enable a consumer to seek redress under the Consumer Rights Act 2015? *(2 marks)*
   (a) The dress purchased did not fit.
   (b) A hairdresser dyed someone's hair orange instead of blonde.
   (c) A new car that had to go back for repairs 4 times in the first 30 days.
   (d) A toy bought from a pound shop that fell apart after 3 months' use.
   (e) A person who wishes to return his iPhone as a newer model is released 2 weeks after purchase.
2. Explain one reason why a business should ensure that they are fully compliant with the latest consumer legislation *(3 marks)*

Chapter review questions

1. What are the three main provisions of the Consumer Rights Act 2015 that relate to the sale of goods?
2. Outline the relevant time restrictions involved when a consumer makes a claim under the consumer rights act?
3. What are the 'protected characteristics' described in the Equality Act 2010?
4. How can a person gain redress when a current or prospective employer is in contravention of the Equality Act 2010?
5. What is the central guiding principle of UK Health and Safety legislation?

Key terms

Acts of Parliament are specific laws made by parliament to change, for example, the rights that individuals' receive in the workplace.

Legislation is the term used to describe all of the laws made by the UK parliament.

Mediation is a method by which parties in conflict with each other can meet to try to come to an agreement acceptable to both sides.

Remedies are the ways in which the legal system offers redress to injured parties, for example, compensation.

Tribunals are set up to hear cases and rule where there are disputes between employers and their employees.

Chapter 1.5.4

The economy and business

Aims

By the end of this chapter, students should be able to understand the impact of the economic climate on businesses in terms of:

- unemployment.
- changing levels of consumer income.
- inflation.
- changes in interest rates.
- government taxation.
- changes in exchange rates.

The impact of the economic climate on businesses

The economic climate refers to the status of the economy at a given time according to the key variables that we use to measure its performance. These variables are:

- **Unemployment** – the level of unemployment is the number of people of working age who are actively searching for work but without a job. Large numbers of unemployed people can be problematic for some businesses but might be an opportunity for others. Businesses selling luxury items in premium markets will find their consumer base eroded and their revenues and profit falling. On the other hand, businesses that are selling low cost items might prosper because of the increased demand from consumers looking to save money. In addition, employees should be easier to find and cheaper to employ as wages fall when jobs are scarce.

Figure 1.5.4a: UK unemployment rate (%)

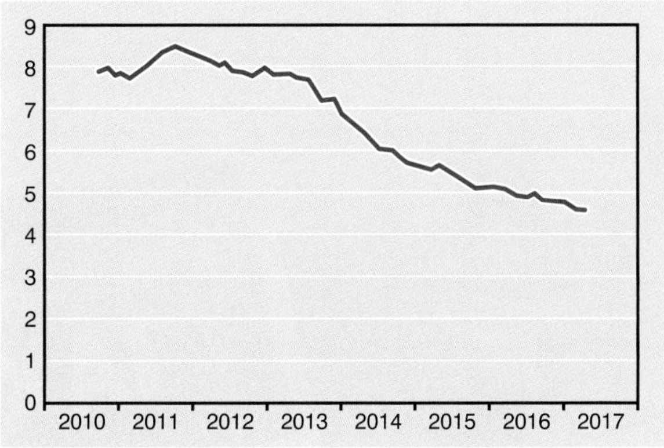

Source: ONS

Figure 1.5.4a shows the reduction in unemployment that has been observed in the UK since 2012. This has been seen as a key achievement of the government and there is little doubt that it has led to rising consumer confidence and higher profits on average.

- **Changing levels of consumer income** will directly impact on the fortunes of most businesses. Wages in the UK remained relatively stagnant between 2010 and 2013 which provided a challenging environment for businesses looking to expand. On the other hand, Aldi and Lidl were able to expand throughout this period.
- **Inflation** is the persistent increase in the average price level in an economy. On the face of it, it might be easy to conclude that a business charging a higher price is a good thing as it will increase profits.

However, there is the distinct possibility that it can harm both revenue and profit levels. In the months after the UK public decided to leave the European Union inflation began to increase and this was predicted to threaten the ability of UK firms to compete internationally. Many businesses will start to see pressures on costs as the costs of supplies start to rise. In addition, when prices in the economy are rising workers try to maintain their living standards by pushing for higher pay.

Figure 1.5.4b: CPI inflation, May 2016 - June 2017 (%)

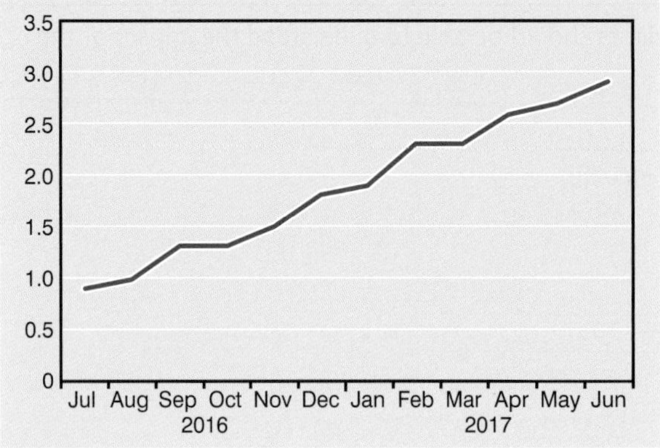

Source: ONS

Figure 1.5.4b shows the increasing rate of inflation since June 2016. Business owners might find controlling cost more challenging if prices continue to rise at this rate.

- **Interest rates** are the cost of borrowing or the reward for saving. Generally speaking, businesses prefer a low interest rate environment where they can borrow to finance investment cheaply and consumers are discouraged from saving. An obvious exception to this are lenders and finance companies who can make money when interest rates rise.
- Government taxation can take many forms but is usually seen as a negative by business and many big businesses can go to great lengths to avoid paying tax through exploiting tax loopholes. **Value added tax** (VAT) is a tax on the sales of most goods and services. The UK rate of VAT is 20% of the price charged and this is usually passed on to consumers. Without VAT, businesses could charge lower prices and earn higher revenues. **Corporation tax** is tax levied on company profits and can be a controversial

Value added tax is a tax on the sales of most goods and services.

tax as it is seen by some as a disincentive to invest and grow a business. In addition, a reduction in income tax levied on individuals could lead to higher revenues for firms now that households have more disposable income.

- The **exchange rate** is the price of one currency expressed in terms of another. UK businesses that try to export goods abroad can suffer if the currency is too strong as it makes the price of their goods expensive in foreign markets. However, a weak currency can spell trouble for a business that is heavily reliant on the import of supplies which are now costlier. After the 2016 Brexit vote the pound sterling saw a significant reduction in its exchange rate. This prompted a welcome rise in exports as our businesses were more competitive in foreign markets but businesses focused primarily on the domestic market will have found this development far less positive due to rising costs of production.

Exam style questions

1. Outline one way in which the economic climate might impact on delivery services such as Deliveroo. *(2 marks)*
2. Analyse the potential impact on the profits of Jaguar Land Rover UK of an increase in the UK exchange rate. *(6 marks)*

Chapter review questions

1. Explain what is meant by the 'economic climate'.
2. Explain the circumstances in which a rise in unemployment could be positive for business.
3. Why might a fall in consumer incomes benefit certain businesses?
4. Explain why inflation can be a problem for the ability of firms to compete in international markets.
5. Why are high interest rates usually a problem for retailers?
6. Why might high rates of income tax and business tax reduce profitability?
7. Why could a reduction in the exchange rate lead to problems for a business?

Key terms

Exchange rates are the price of one currency expressed in terms of another.

Inflation is a sustained rise in the average level of prices in the economy.

Interest rates are the cost of borrowing money or the reward for saving.

Unemployment is the number of people of working age who are actively searching for work but without a job.

Chapter 1.5.5

External influences

Aims

By the end of this chapter, students should be able to:

- understand the importance of external influences on business.
- understand how a business might respond to changes in: technology, legislation and the economic climate.

The importance of external influences on business

Businesses can and should focus on making their internal organisation more efficient and dynamic but it is equally important to pay attention to the environment in which the business operates. Business that can adapt to a changing marketplace, new disruptive technologies and economic upheaval will find themselves able to evolve and prosper. Toyota are an example of a business that has embraced new technologies and changing customer preferences to gain a competitive advantage in the production of hybrid vehicles. All car makers are using technology to add features such as navigation and communications technology to their dashboards and the race is now on to build the first self-driving car. However, selling these goods in a slowing global economy might be a challenge if they cannot produce the goods at the right price. External influences matter a great deal.

Influence of technological change on business

Technology has transformed the way businesses operate, communicate, order supplies and research their competitors and the potential market. Technology has also transformed the way people buy goods and services and access information. The introduction of technology has created both new jobs and made some jobs redundant. For example, the increase in internet banking has meant that less people are required to serve people in banks but more people are required to design software for the bank to use, to train employees how to use it and to service the hardware.

Technology can influence businesses in a number of positive ways:

- Use of email, social media and instant messaging makes communication with staff and customers easier and more timely.
- The internet enables businesses to easily carry out market research.
- The use of machinery such as robots means that labour costs may be reduced.
- A computerised quality control system in a factory may improve the quality of goods produced.
- Many processes can be automated e.g. money counting machines in banks and stock control in supermarkets. Therefore, more customers can be served in a time period and costs of production may fall.
- Recruitment interviews can take place using software such as Skype, which is free, and this reduces the recruitment costs.
- Introduction of new technology creates opportunities for businesses to provide associated products and services. For example, smartphones have created a need for applications to run on the phones, new devices need cases, adaptors and cables, whilst cafes can offer free wireless internet access to attract smartphone or laptop users.
- Businesses can exist on the internet (e-business) and therefore do not need to rent retail premises and this reduces costs.
- Businesses can access global markets via online shops. This means they can access suppliers and be accessed by customers located throughout the world. This increases potential markets and may reduce costs.

- Large amounts of information can be shared quickly and conveniently between employees and other branches of the business located worldwide.

Technology can influence businesses in a number of negative ways:

- Advancements in technology mean that businesses have to adapt to a constantly changing environment and this process of change needs to be managed carefully. Uber is a clear example of how technology can disrupt a market and threaten the success of existing suppliers.
- Technology can quickly become out-of-date and replacing equipment can be costly. If it is not replaced, then parts and complementary goods can be difficult to buy.
- Workers need to be trained to use new technology and in the short run this is costly and time-consuming.
- Advancements in technology can damage the business of some firms e.g. Waterstones has faced fierce competition from online booksellers who do not have to cover the costs of providing a high street retail space.

Influence of legislation on business

Chapter 1.5.3 looks at some of the key legislation that impacts on UK businesses but it is not just consumer and employment law that businesses must be aware of. Changes in many different areas of law are likely to have an impact on UK businesses.

Examples of how recent legislation has impacted on businesses:

- A recent change in the penalty points that a driver is handed for mobile phone use at the wheel may provide a boost in demand for car hands-free kits.
- Ever tighter legislation with regard to smoking tobacco has led to tobacco firms seeking out new overseas markets and investing in research and development to find a 'safe' form of smoking.
- The European Union Act 2017 which permitted the activation of Article 50 of the Lisbon Treaty will have signalled severe implications for those businesses that sell significant volumes of goods to the EU or rely on EU firms for supplies. A period of planning for our secession will be at the forefront of the agenda of many businesses before 2019.

A recent change in the penalty points that a driver is handed for mobile phone use at the wheel may provide a boost in demand for car hands-free kits.

- The Psychoactive Substances Act 2016 banned the sale of so called 'legal highs' and put many shops that sold such substances out of business. Unfortunately, this has had the consequence of driving the sale of these drugs into the informal market.

Influence of the economic climate on business

The economy influences businesses in many ways. Chapter 1.5.4 deals with this in detail but the following influences are likely to have the most profound impact on businesses operating in the UK:

- If the economy is in a period of economic growth it may be favourable for many businesses.
- If the economy is experiencing negative growth it may be unfavourable for many businesses.
- An increase/decrease in government spending will impact upon many businesses.
- A change in interest and/or tax rates will impact upon many businesses.
- A change in exchange rates will have an effect on businesses which trade overseas.

Exam style question 1

Amazon have been investing in research for delivery drones. It is thought that this technology could revolutionise the UK marketplace.

1. Explain an external influence *other than changes in technology* that Amazon faces. *(3 marks)*
2. Analyse the impact on Amazon of the development of fully operational delivery drones. *(6 marks)*

Exam style question 2

Nissan are a Japanese car manufacturer that produce cars for the European market in Sunderland, Tyne and Wear. The Brexit legislation is likely to mean that Nissan will face difficulties in exporting to the EU in the future. In addition, the decision to leave the EU has meant a significant reduction in the value of Sterling.

1. Explain why a fall in the value of Sterling might be advantageous for Nissan. *(3 marks)*
2. Analyse how the decision to exit the EU could impact negatively on the profits of Nissan. *(6 marks)*

Chapter review questions

1. Explain 2 ways in which each of the following can influence business decisions:
   (a) Technology.
   (b) Legislation.
   (c) Economic issues.
2. Give an example of a newly introduced tax and explain how its actions impacted upon a business.
3. Explain how Twitter and Facebook have changed the ways in which business is conducted in the UK.

Key terms

Economic issues are those associated with the state of the economy and government economic policy.

Legislation refers to the passing of laws in parliament. Changes in the law will often mean that businesses can, should or must change the way they do business.

Technological issues involve the use of existing and new technologies and their impact on how businesses function.

Chapter 2.1.1

Business growth

Aims

By the end of this chapter, students should be able to understand:

- methods of business growth and their impact: internal and external growth.
- the types of business ownership for growing businesses.
- sources of finance for growing and established businesses.

Internal (organic) growth

Internal or **organic growth** is where a business grows through expansion of their existing operations. This might be through launching a new product or finding new markets to sell to. Internal growth is seen as the least risky type of growth. The gradual nature of expansion may allow for better control for the owners and timely evaluation of performance as the company enters new markets or starts new ventures.

Internal growth can occur through launching **new products**. Apple stared life in the 1970s as a business that designed and produced computer hardware. It has grown to the corporate giant that it is today by continually researching and developing innovative new products such as the iPhone (first launched in June 2007) and the Apple Watch (first launched in April 2015).

Internal growth can occur through expanding into **new markets**. Netflix has seen stunning growth since it began streaming media in 2007 and is a strong example of how a business can quickly expand overseas. By 2017, Netflix had expanded across the globe and now only China, the Democratic People's Republic of Korea, Syria and the Crimea do not have access to its content.

LEGO® has moved into new markets through its creation of cartoons such as Ninjago and through their LEGO® films. Not only were the films profitable at the box office, they have also successfully enabled them to capitalise on their new found popularity with a new generation. This is a good example of a company which has changed its marketing mix (a new kind of promotion and expanding the product range) in order to help with expansion in overseas markets. LEGO® has also taken advantage of technology in its introduction of LEGO® Education which encourages children to learn coding and robotics through using LEGO® software programmes made for schools.

External (inorganic) growth

External growth can be achieved when a business joins with another business. This is often a quicker means of growth than internal growth and newly created companies can make spectacular gains in market share overnight. However, the benefits of growing at such speed such as increased pricing power and lower costs of production must be balanced against the pitfalls of joining two different companies together. There are no guarantees that the two businesses are compatible and that the predicted benefits will be achieved.

Methods of external growth include the following:

Mergers

A merger can be defined as two existing businesses joining to form one larger business. Joining existing businesses together can be a quicker way of expanding the size and scope of a business. A good example of a merger was the joining together of Dixons and Carphone Warehouse in 2014 to create a high street powerhouse incorporating those two brands plus PC World. Another example of such a situation is where T-Mobile and Orange merged to form the larger mobile network Everything Everywhere (EE) in 2010. This merger created a larger network which, for example, might have simultaneously provided greater market power and falling costs due to enhanced purchasing power.

Takeovers

A takeover is where one business assumes control of another business, usually through acquiring a controlling interest, i.e. owning the majority of the share capital of a company. BT staged a controversial £12.5bn takeover of EE in 2016. This led to the telecommunications company having a large share of the market in both landline and mobile telephone provision. It also allows the two companies involved to share good ideas and cut costs through a process of rationalisation of the workforce. Takeovers do not always work out as planned, however. When RBS acquired the Dutch bank ABN-AMRO in 2008 they did so at the peak of the market and paid a premium for doing so. In addition, their valuation was far in excess of what it would have been had they known about all of the weak assets held by the target bank. When takeovers such as this go wrong they can threaten the existence of both companies.

The types of business ownership for growing businesses: public limited company (plc)

A public limited company (PLC) is a limited liability company that has its shares traded publicly on the London Stock Exchange rather than privately (see Chapter 1.4.1). When the business offers their shares for sale in this way it gives firms access to a much wider investor base. These large injections of funds can enable a business to achieve strong growth. It can finance the research and development of new products, the purchase of new premises, the adoption of new capital machinery or the sort of marketing spending that will allow for penetration into new markets.

Sources of finance for growing and established businesses: internal sources

Retained profit – profit which is kept back from being paid to the shareholders as dividends can be reinvested into the company. Google is a good example of a business which has a strong record of reinvesting profits to further grow the company and to diversify into new areas. What was just a search engine earning income from online advertising has diversified through: the Android operating system, the acquisition of YouTube and the Google Play store that sells media content.

Selling assets – Businesses that have assets are able to sell them off and use the money to grow the business. Assets can include brands, buildings and capital machinery. In 2017 Unilever put the Flora and Stork brands up for sale in a bid to generate £6bn that could be reinvested elsewhere.

Sources of finance for growing and established businesses: external sources

Loan capital – banks are usually eager to lend to large businesses due to their lower risk profile and the size of the loans involved. As a result, low interest rates are often offered which can lead to relatively cheap financing of investment projects. As discussed in Chapter 1.3.4, there are drawbacks to using this type of finance which are that the interest paid on the loan will increase business costs and, if the business is already in a significant amount of debt, there might not be any willing lenders.

Share capital – when a firm transitions from a private limited company (Ltd) to a public limited company (PLC), it does so by selling shares via an initial public offering (IPO). A prospectus is produced and the shares are offered at an initial price set by the company which reflects the owners' valuation of it. After the IPO, the value of the company is determined by the price the shares are trading for on the LSE (London Stock Exchange).

Banks are usually eager to lend to large businesses due to their lower risk profile and the size of the loans involved.

This process is known as '**flotation**' and selling shares in this manner gives the business access to wealthy individual investors and institutional investors such as pension funds. Large amounts of capital can therefore be raised to finance investment in machinery, marketing, and the setting up of new outlets to facilitate expansion. The key drawback of selling off a large portion of your business in this way is that you will have sold off a claim to the future profits earned. For most business owners, however, a smaller share in a larger and more profitable business is better than a majority share in a business without sufficient finance to grow.

Exam style question

Eddie Stobart is a haulage and logistics company based in the UK. It began life in the 1970s as a small family business in the North of England but has grown through expanding its scope to the rest of the UK and Europe and using profits to expand its fleet of lorries. In 2017 it is considering a stock market flotation in an initial public offering that would value the business at around £550m.

1. Define the term 'stock market flotation'. *(1 mark)*
2. Discuss whether a stock market flotation is the best method of financing further growth at Eddie Stobart. *(6 marks)*

Chapter review questions

1. Explain what is meant by internal growth.
2. Outline two ways that a firm can grow using internal growth.
3. Explain what is meant by external growth
4. Why can mergers and takeovers go wrong?
5. State two sources of internal finance.
6. State two sources of external finance.
7. What is meant by the term 'public limited company'?
8. Explain why a large firm might prefer to use loan capital rather than sell shares via the stock market.

Key terms

External growth is where a business grows through joining with another separate company.

Internal growth is where a business grows through expansion of their existing operations.

IPO is an initial public offering when a private limited company sells shares on the stock market for the first time.

Mergers occur when two businesses voluntarily join together to form a single business.

Public limited companies are limited liability companies whose shares can be traded publicly through the stock market.

Retained profit is profit which is kept back from being paid to the shareholders and as dividends can be reinvested into the company.

Share capital describes the money raised by a firm through selling shares.

Takeovers occur when one business assumes control of another business, usually through acquiring a controlling interest via the purchase of shares.

Chapter 2.1.2

Changes in business aims and objectives

Aims

By the end of this chapter, students should be able to understand:

- why business aims and objectives change as businesses evolve.
- how business aims and objectives change as businesses evolve.

Why business aims and objectives change

Business aims and objectives (see Chapter 1.3.1) guide the actions of a business and change in response to changes in the external and internal business environments in which the organisation operates:

- **Changes in the external environment** include: changes in market conditions, technology and legislation.
- **Changes in internal factors** include: changes in the performance of the business, changes in staffing and the skills and expertise of those leaving or joining, and changes to production processes.

Aims are the purpose of a business and what it hopes to achieve. **Objectives** are the medium to long term targets of a business organisation, e.g. survival, growth, market share, wealth creation and profitability.

Market conditions, such as increased competition or a decrease in demand for a business's goods and services, may bring about changes in aims and objectives. As more firms enter a market and competition increases, a business may change its objectives from being a market leader to retaining its market share.

For example, a major airline may find itself under threat from budget airlines flying similar routes. This may force the airline to reconsider its objective of being a market leader on certain routes to retaining its existing customers.

Technology can change the aims and objectives of a business. For example, a business may change from using traditional payment methods to embracing internet technologies and being innovative. For example, Starbucks now has an app that enables its customers to order coffee in advance, pay online and therefore skip the queue and collect their order at the agreed time from the collection counter. Rivals that do not offer the same level of service may lose customers, so it is necessary to adapt its objectives to accommodate changes and keep abreast with competitors.

Legislation may cause a business to adopt more environmentally friendly practices to retain customers and attract new ones. Coca-Cola has heavily promoted Cola-Cola Zero (sugar free) in the UK in an attempt to cushion the impact of the sugar tax (April 2018). The American company aims to have over half of its annual sales in the UK to consist of sugar free and low sugar versions to minimise the threat of a sugar tax, which could reduce sales.

Poor performance will result in a fall in profits, so may cause business objectives to change from maintaining market share to survival. A business like McDonald's has to adapt to retain its market share. Technology in the form of self-service screens and contactless debit cards and Apple Pay has allowed McDonald's to maintain its market share and keep up with competitors. Innovations can sustain an interest in the products of a business, such as the novelty of McDonald's 'create your own burger' using interactive ordering and self-payment systems.

Internal factors that impact on changes in aims and objectives include changes in staffing. For instance, a new Managing Director or Chief Executive Officer joining the company can create a change in the firm's aims and objectives. A firm with a high staff turnover rate (see Chapter 2.5.2) may question its objectives and refocus on retaining its employees. A change in production processes, such as the use of technologies in a restaurant, will also change the aims and objectives in terms of training and staffing needs.

How business aims and objectives change

As a business grows and evolves, its aims and objectives will tend to change.

Focus on survival or growth

A business in the early stages of its life may have **survival** as it main aim. As it acquires customers and sales revenues increase, the aims and objectives may change to increasing market share, growth or maximising sales revenue. For example, Fjällräven is a Swedish outdoor clothing firm which started making clothes in a basement of the founder's home in 1960. It now sells clothing in over thirty countries. In the beginning, Fjällräven's objective may have been survival, but this changed to growth as the business entered new markets later on in its life.

Entering or exiting markets

Blackberry was once a popular phone amongst business executives, with its own operating system, mini keyboard and encrypted messages which meant that they could not be intercepted. The company had significant market share. However, the entrance of Apple's iPhone and Samsung's smartphones eroded Blackberry's market share. Matters were made worse when client data was exposed, and since then Blackberry has battled to survive. Blackberry as a business has had to adapt to its changing circumstances, with its objective of higher market share changed to business survival.

Sometimes a business may exit a market because it is facing a decrease in customers. Krispy Kreme Donuts entered the Hong Kong market but only survived for a few years because it did not gain popularity in this market. Objectives of growth and increasing market share changed to business survival, and eventually the exit of Krispy Kreme Donuts from Hong Kong.

Growing or reducing the workforce

A growing business will need to increase its workforce to meet rising demand. A school, for example, may need to increase the number of qualified staff to meet the growing popularity of its BTEC courses in Art and Design and Sports Science. On the other hand, a school facing budget cuts may have to change its aims and objectives from providing a broad range of subjects, courses and extra-curricular activities to having a more focused approach by dropping less popular subjects. Recently some airlines have had to cut staff due to falling sales revenue and increasing competition. Their objectives may change from retaining market share to cost reduction and business survival.

Krispy Kreme Donuts entered the Hong Kong market but only survived for a few years because it did not gain popularity in this market.

Increasing or decreasing the product range

A business may decide to increase or decrease its product range and this may impact business objectives. Amazon started out as an online book seller and then vastly expanded the number of products sold to what it is today – a giant online retailer. Zara originally specialised in being a clothing retailer but has expanded its product range to include Zara Home.

Crocs shoes started by selling shoes made out of foam on a small scale and rapid success and popularity of the shoe encouraged it to broaden its product range and create sandals, Wellington boots, and slippers which are sold in its own Crocs shops in a large number of countries. The objectives of Crocs changed from increasing market share to entering new overseas markets and increasing the product range. By contrast, Tesco cut its product range by offering less choice for standard products such as tomato ketchup. It did this to compete with low cost rivals such as Aldi and Lidl that carry a smaller product range to cut costs.

Exam style question

Identify and justify a possible change in objectives for the following businesses:

(a) A long established national airline facing competition from a budget airline. *(2 marks)*

(b) A well-known UK supermarket facing competition from cheaper European rivals. *(2 marks)*

(c) A small independent health food shop facing increased competition from mainstream supermarkets increasing their range of organic, vegan and gluten free foods. *(2 marks)*

Chapter review questions

1. Give two examples of market conditions which could impact objectives of a business.
2. Explain how technology may change business objectives.
3. Give an example of what may cause business objectives to change from survival to growth.
4. Explain how legislation may impact business objectives.
5. State three different objectives a business may have over its life.
6. What are the reasons why a business may reduce its product range?
7. State two reasons why a business may enter a new market.
8. Why might a business exit a market?

Key terms

Aims are the purpose of a business and what it hopes to achieve.

Objectives are the medium to long term targets of a business organisation, e.g. survival, growth, market share, wealth creation and profitability.

Chapter 2.1.3

Business and globalisation

Aims

By the end of this chapter, students should be able to understand:

- the impact of globalisation on businesses.
- barriers to international trade.
- how businesses compete internationally.

Globalisation

Globalisation is the process of ever-closer integration of the global economy. It involves the freer movement of:

- Goods and services
- Capital
- Labour
- Information

Globalisation has accelerated over the past 25 years due to factors such as the information revolution, the rise of the container ship, the trend for emerging economies to embrace free trade and the falling cost of international travel (in real terms at least).

The impact of globalisation on business: imports

The freer movement of goods and services means that domestic businesses are exposed to a greater level of **competition from foreign imports**. This has led to severe difficulties for some firms. In 2016, for example, Tata steel in the UK was close to business failure due to the large amount of cheap Chinese steel on the global market. The firms that have managed to cope with the extra levels of competition have been forced to pay closer attention to controlling costs and competing harder for business than ever before.

On the other hand, those businesses that have relied on **imports** of raw materials, semi-finished goods or capital equipment have been able to source their goods from a wider range of suppliers. The new global marketplace has led to UK businesses being able to find cheaper alternatives to their existing suppliers and reduce their costs as a result.

The impact of globalisation on business: exports

As globalisation has gathered pace, countries such as India, China and the emerging markets of South East Asia have started to open themselves up to trade. In doing so they have developed their economies and transitioned from low income to middle income economies. This has presented some wonderful opportunities for UK businesses. For example, our financial services exports are used throughout the world and our manufactured goods such as Land Rovers and Minis now compete in an increasing number of car markets.

The impact of globalisation on business: changing business locations

An increasingly globalised world has meant that firms with vision have been able to take advantage of a large increase in the options in terms of where to locate businesses. Businesses no longer need to export goods from one country to the rest of the world – they have the opportunity to choose a number of regional hubs and can select the country where a quality product can be made at a cheaper cost. European car makers have taken advantage of the accession of Eastern European countries such as Poland to the EU and have produced goods there to export to the rest of the EU single market and beyond.

The emerging economies such as China have, in many ways, become the world's production line and developed economies like the UK have focused on producing services. Rapid technological progress has also meant that service firms such as accountants or consultancy firms have the opportunity to locate themselves anywhere as a physical base is less important to doing business as a strong online presence.

The impact of globalisation on business: multinationals

A multinational corporation is any company that has business operations in more than one country. HSBC is a good example of such a corporation with its large presence in London and Hong Kong to name just two countries where it does business. Multinationals are able to benefit from lower costs due to their large size, wield a greater market power due to their recognisable brand names and are able to spread risk as they operate in a number of economic environments. Multinationals that produce goods such as Samsung are able to set up a global supply chain whereby the different stages of production take place in the most suitable part of the world. For example, the design of a new smartphone might take place in California but the mass production of the product could take place in China where labour costs are a fraction of what they are in the USA.

Barriers to international trade

- **Tariffs** are taxes applied on imports. They are usually put in place to discourage consumers from buying imports and to provide an incentive to consume domestic goods and can be thought of as a barrier against free international trade. For example, the EU placed tariffs on solar panel imports from China in 2013 to protect the market for EU producers.
- **Trade blocs** are groups of countries (usually in a geographical region) that protect themselves against imports with a common external tariff placed on goods coming into the bloc. This means that when the EU decides to put tariffs on solar panels the tariff charged is the same no matter where in the EU the goods arrive.

How businesses compete internationally: the use of the internet and e-commerce

E-commerce can be defined as commercial transactions conducted on the internet. Businesses can use the internet to compete in markets that might be hundreds or even thousands of miles away. The internet has opened up new possibilities and markets for businesses which can now market their products via advertising online and through search engines. This means that consumers from across the world can be alerted to your products or services and can make payment to you via a credit card from anywhere at any time. In addition, forging and building relationships with consumers is made possible through email and via social media. Finally, new media technologies such as streaming have changed the nature of some markets from a local market such as the market for the hire of physical media such as DVDs to a global streaming market dominated by the likes of Amazon Prime.

Changing the marketing mix to compete internationally

Product – firms that are competing in international markets will, naturally, have to pay careful attention to the prevailing cultural norms in their target market. For example, banks that are attempting to move into countries with a predominantly Muslim population will need to provide banking products that are in accordance with Islamic laws regarding the charging of interest.

Price – In a country where the market that a business is selling in is already saturated the management may opt to use competitive pricing. However, moving into a country with no genuine competition may provide the opportunity to use skim pricing.

Promotion – A business that wishes to promote their product in the UK or Ireland may find that buying an advertising slot in the break of a soap opera is a great way to build brand awareness. However, in countries with a more outdoors-based lifestyle such as Australia this strategy might not be as successful.

Place – selling goods online to be delivered might work well in the UK and the USA where internet services are fast and reliable, there is strong transport infrastructure and people put a great value on their time. However, other distribution channels are likely to make more sense in a country like Thailand where the situation with regard to these factors is markedly different.

Exam style question 1

Red Bus Shop is a family-owned chain of UK and London themed souvenir and gift shops which are located close to the main London tourist sites such as the London Eye. They source a lot of their supplies from manufacturers based in China. Their employees come from all over Europe.

1. Define the term 'imports'. *(1 mark)*
2. Explain how globalisation might have impacted on their costs. *(3 marks)*
3. Explain how globalisation might have impacted on their revenues. *(3 marks)*
4. Discuss whether or not Red Bus Shop should close down their retail outlets and focus on e-commerce instead. *(6 marks)*

Chapter review questions

1. Define 'globalisation'.
2. What factors have led to an increasingly globalised world in the last three decades?
3. Explain how firms can benefit from an increased range of imports.
4. Explain how firms can benefit when new export markets are opened up.
5. What is a multinational corporation?
6. Explain why companies such as Apple can take advantage of an increasingly globalised world economy.
7. Explain why tariffs might help UK businesses.
8. What is a trade bloc?
9. How can firms use e-commerce to increase their competitiveness in international markets?
10. In what two ways might a breakfast cereal manufacturer need to change the marketing mix in order to enter a new market?

Key terms

E-commerce refers to commercial transactions conducted on the internet.

Exports are sales made to consumers, firms or governments based overseas.

Globalisation is the process of ever-closer integration of the global economy.

Imports are goods that are bought from businesses based overseas.

Multinationals are businesses that operate in more than one country.

Tariffs are taxes imposed on imports in order to raise their prices and reduce their demand.

Trade blocs are groups of countries that protect themselves against imports with a common external tariff placed on goods coming into the bloc.

Chapter 2.1.4

Ethics, the environment and business

Aims

By the end of this chapter, students should be able to understand:

- the impact of ethical and environmental considerations on businesses.
- how ethical considerations influence business activity.
- how environmental considerations influence business activity.
- the potential impact of pressure group activity on the marketing mix.

Influence of ethical considerations on business activity: possible trade-offs between ethics and profit

Ethics are described as a system of moral values and therefore an **ethical business** can be described as one which bases its decisions on underlying principles and values. Businesses try to act ethically to satisfy the needs of their stakeholders.

The Body Shop is an example of a business which states that it is 'against animal testing' on the labels of its products and it therefore may be considered to be an ethical business. L'Occitane, a premium priced producer of cosmetics and beauty products, trains visually impaired people in France to acquire skills that will help them to gain employment. It also purchases shea butter, an essential ingredient for several of their products, produced by women in Burkina Faso. The women are paid a price for the shea butter that covers production costs, environmental and social costs and also leaves a profit which can be invested in to the local community. L'Occitane may therefore also be considered to be an ethical company.

Ethical issues influence businesses in a number of positive ways:

- Businesses with ethical principles respect their employees and the community in which they operate.
- Businesses may endeavour to educate young people and the general public and therefore benefit society.
- Ethical businesses may also uphold principles of sustainable development and may ensure that their actions cause minimal negative impact on the environment. This may enhance the positive image of the business and boost sales and profits.

Ethical issues influence businesses in a number of negative ways:

- If a business acts unethically, for example, uses child labour in the manufacturing of its products or exploits workers by not paying a fair price for their efforts then its activities may be reported in the media and this would be bad for the company's reputation and lead to a drop in sales.
- If a business claimed that its products were not tested on animals but essential ingredients had in the past been tested on animals, then it would be acting unethically. This might damage its reputation and cause a subsequent drop in sales if the welfare of animals was compromised.

As discussed, businesses have both a positive and negative impact on society. An interesting debate is whether businesses are contributing to society in an attempt to compensate for some of the negative impacts they have on society or whether it is merely a public relations exercise designed to enhance the brand in the eyes of the consumer. In reality, it is possibly a combination of both motives.

Acting ethically can often lead to increased costs. L'Occitane's shea butter could, no doubt, be sourced more cheaply from less ethical sources. This raises the question of whether acting ethically presents a **trade-off** with profitability. It is certainly possible that this might be the case. However, firms that have ethical consumers are likely to be able to attract a large amount of ethical consumers who have strong brand loyalty and are less price-sensitive. This means that the firm might be positioned to earn significantly more revenue and higher profits as a result.

L'Occitane may be considered to be an ethical company.

Exam style question 1

People Tree is a UK based clothing company that makes garments from materials sourced from 15 different countries. All materials are purchased on a fair trade basis and any services, for example, embroidery, stitching and weaving are also paid for on a fair trade basis. This means that the prices of the garments are pitched at a level which covers production costs and allows the producers to make a profit instead of being based on the global market price for that material as this can often be less than the production costs. This arrangement makes it possible for profits of trade to be fed back into the community. The methods of production are all designed to minimise the impact on the environment, for example all dyes used are natural.

Source: Adapted from www.peopletree.co.uk

(a) Identify two ways in which People Tree operates on ethical principles. *(2 marks)*

(b) Discuss how ethical principles can influence a business. *(6 marks)*

Influence of environmental issues and sustainability on business: possible trade-offs between the environment, sustainability and profit

Sustainable economic development is economic development which satisfies current needs but does not use up the earth's resources so that the needs of future generations are compromised. Many governments are putting strategies in place to ensure that businesses act responsibly.

The trend of caring for the environment has increased demand for environmentally friendly cleaning products, biodegradable plastic bags, recycling bins and products with recycled packaging. Businesses have had to adapt to meet the needs of their customers and have had to introduce ways of reducing waste, recycling and making sure that their actions have minimal impact on the environment.

Technology has caused patterns of consumer expenditure to change, for example, people send fewer Christmas cards preferring instead to send an 'e-greeting' or post a message on Facebook. The fall in demand for Christmas cards could be because of lower household incomes, a decrease in spending, an increase in the cost of postage, a change in how people communicate and, in some cases, a concern for the environment.

Environmental issues can influence businesses in a number of positive ways:

- Some businesses have started to take responsibility for their own actions and therefore, for example, try to minimise waste, reduce their use of electricity and recycle resources.
- There has been a sharp increase in the understanding of environmental issues which has caused businesses to respond to the demands of the market and act in a more environmentally responsible manner. For example, many businesses now use recycled paper for their correspondence. M·A·C, a cosmetics manufacturer and retailer offers a discount to customers who return old lipstick containers for recycling when they make a purchase.
- Some businesses have started to use more renewable energy sources, for example solar power.
- In many countries, for example, Australia, USA and the UK, many new buildings are designed to reduce their impact on the environment in terms of energy use, water efficiency and the materials and resources used.

Environmental issues can influence businesses in a number of negative ways:

- If a business does not act responsibly and, for example, pollutes a river with waste then it may be criticised in the media which may damage its reputation and reduce sales.
- Businesses may lose environmentally conscious customers if they do not implement environmentally friendly initiatives like their competitors.
- Some businesses introduce products and actively promote them and therefore encourage consumption of goods and services, which can create wastage and be a strain on resources.

Acting in a more sustainable manner can be costly for a business and harm profit margins. This **trade-off** is especially the case in the short run as, for example, energy from renewable sources might be costlier than 'dirty' fuel generated from coal or gas. However, it is also the case that a focus on minimising the waste of resources can become part of a drive for leaner production which will reduce costs overall. Furthermore, environmentally conscious consumers are likely to be loyal to businesses which take sustainability seriously and, again, they are likely to be prepared to pay higher prices. It is quite possible, therefore, that a focus on being environmentally friendly could lead to higher profits in the long run.

Exam style question 2

Pret a Manger is a food retailer and café popular in the UK and parts of Europe. Its website speaks of the business having "a strategic approach to reduce its impact on the environment, and to have a positive impact on the society it operates in." Its policy on resource use is that it is "committed to reducing our embedded carbon, making waste useful and using less resource in the things that we consume."

Source Adapted from: www.pret.co.uk

(a) Explain one way in which care for the environment impacts upon the way Pret a Manger operates. *(3 marks)*

(b) Discuss the following statement, 'Pret a Manger makes a positive contribution to society'. *(6 marks)*

The potential impact of pressure groups on the marketing mix

Pressure groups are groups of like-minded individuals who work together to put pressure on businesses and/or governments for change that benefits society. Possible impacts of pressure groups on the marketing mix include:

- Preventing manufacturers or retailers of alcoholic drinks from using sales **promotions**.
- Lobbying the government to put a **price** cap on the 'Big 6' energy companies.
- Preventing the location of a nightclub or bar in a **place** such as a residential area.

- Preventing the location (**place**) of a chicken shop near a school.
- Action on Smoking and Health (ASH) is a UK based anti-smoking pressure group that puts pressure on the government to ban smoking in public places and to regulate the sale and advertising of tobacco **products**.

Chapter review questions

1. Explain two ways in which each of the following can influence business decisions:
   (a) ethical issues.
   (b) environmental issues.
2. Give an example of an ethical company and explain the extent to which it deserves this title.
3. Give an example of a pressure group and explain how its actions impacted upon the marketing mix of a business.

Key terms

Environmental issues are concerned with how production and consumption of goods and services affects the natural environment.

An **ethical** business is one which bases its decisions on underlying moral principles and values.

Fair trade is when producers are paid a price for their goods which covers the costs of production and allows the producers to make a profit, which may be reinvested into the local community. This is in contrast to being paid a price based on the global market price as this can often be less than the production costs.

Pressure groups are groups of like-minded individuals who work together to put pressure on businesses and/or governments for change for the betterment of society.

Sustainable economic development is economic development which satisfies current needs and does not use up the earth's resources so that future development is compromised.

Chapter 2.2.1

Product

Aims

By the end of this chapter, students should be able to understand:

- the design mix.
- the product life cycle.
- the importance to a business of differentiating a product/service.

The design mix: function, aesthetics, cost

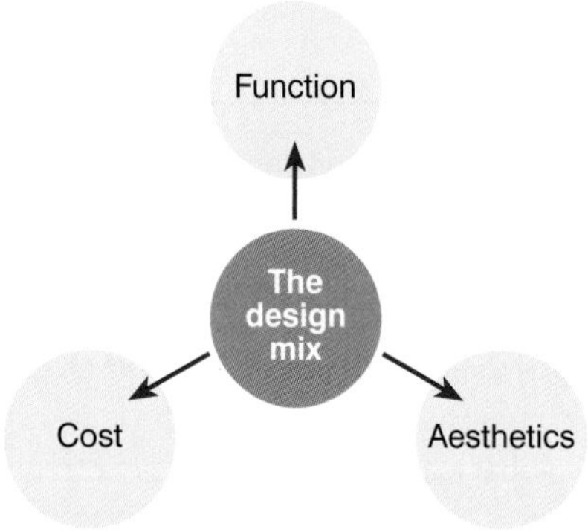

When a business designs a product, it must consider each aspect of the design mix:

- The **function** of a product is concerned with what the product is designed to do, how well it carries out this purpose and how long the product will last.
- The **aesthetics** of a product refers to the style of the product and how the design may attract different customers.
- The **cost** of a product refers to the cost of production. This will directly affect the firm's price, sales, profitability and amount of value added created (see Chapter 1.1.3).

For example, a toaster should be functional, durable and long lasting. The emphasis of this toaster may be on **function**. An example would be a brand of toaster which is well-known for being reliable, such as Phillips or Kenwood. Their prices tend to be mid-range.

A rival toaster may place more emphasis on **aesthetics** than function and although the machine toasts bread it may be retro in design or be an interesting colour. The emphasis is placed on looks rather than on functionality. Examples of such brands are Duralit and Smeg who produce retro toasters in a range of pastel colours. Their prices tend to be high.

Another toaster brand may be produced for the lowest possible **cost**, offering customers value for money. This takes priority over function and aesthetics. This type of toaster again will fulfill its function but may have a shorter life span and be less attractive to look at. An example would be a supermarket own-brand toaster.

The product life cycle

From their initial conception and development to when they are withdrawn, all products go through four distinct stages: launch, growth, maturity and decline. This process is known as the **product life cycle**.

Figure 2.2.1a – The product life cycle

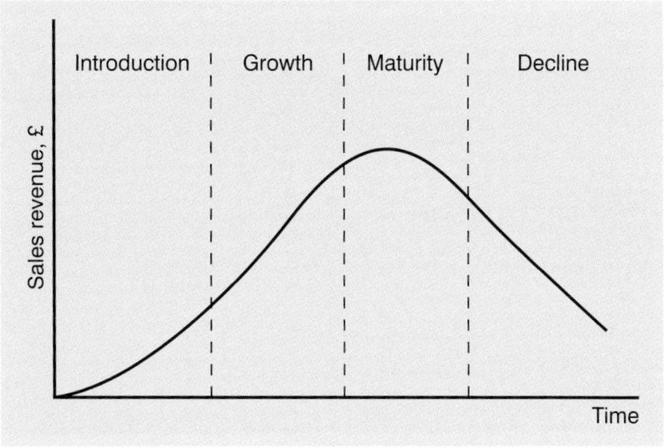

- **Research and development** (not shown on diagram) – During this phase an initial idea for a product occurs and market research takes place. In many cases a prototype is made and may be test marketed on a sample of customers. Modifications may take place in response to market research and findings from test marketing.

- **Launch (Introduction)** – During this phase, most businesses spend large sums on developing, testing, launching and marketing the product. It may begin with a small batch of the products and carry out a launch on a small sample of consumers in order to establish whether the product is likely to thrive. The product may be adapted or aimed at a new market segment as a result of the feedback from consumers of the initial model, or it may be dropped completely.

- **Growth** – This phase is characterised by increased sales as the product starts to take off due to effective marketing (such as a successful advertising campaign and sales promotion). If the test marketing was successful then the product may be rolled out nationally, which again should bring steady sales growth. Cash flow pressures should be eased as sales revenue rises.

- **Maturity** – During the maturity phase, the sales of the product will peak due to increased awareness of the product and the establishment of consumer loyalty. Sales revenue should be high and profits will be at their highest. Successful products strive to remain in this phase as long as possible due to the high profits. For example, brands such as Coca-Cola, Colgate and Oxo have remained mature products for many decades.

- **Decline** – During the final stage of the product life-cycle, sales are falling. The product may have gone out of fashion or competitors may have launched superior products. Generally, businesses will try to sell off remaining stocks at a low price and so the profits made during this phase are low. Businesses are then faced with a decision as to whether to update and reinvent the product or withdraw it.

Extension strategies

If a business can see that its product sales are falling, it may use an **extension strategy** to prolong the maturity phase. These strategies include:

- Producing a new or improved version, such as Apple regularly launching a new version of the iPhone.
- Finding new uses for a product, e.g. promoting baking soda as a natural cleaning product.
- Targeting new market segments, e.g. Lego aimed the 'Friends' range at girls.
- Adapting marketing strategies to reignite demand for the product and to sell it more effectively.

Nike is a readily identifiable sportswear brand due to its catchy name, it's 'tick' logo and its slogan – 'Just Do It'.

The importance of differentiating a product/service

Businesses want their products to be easily identifiable. They also usually want to distinguish their products from that of the competition. This is mostly done through the use of **branding** which is where a name or symbol is given to a product or business as a whole. For example, Nike is a readily identifiable sportswear brand due to its catchy name, it's 'tick' logo and its slogan – 'Just Do It'.

Differentiating a product through branding can be very beneficial for a business because it allows it more freedom to set price, encourages brand loyalty and makes expanding into new markets much easier. Nike started off as a sports shoe brand but the strength of its branding and marketing meant that diversifying into sports equipment and clothing was simpler because the brand was recognised and trusted by their customer base. Other ways a business can differentiate itself from its competitors include selling the product in more or different types of outlets, establishing superior **after-sales services** (such as warranties and technical support) or increasing the product quality (see Chapter 2.3.3).

It is rare, though not unheard of, for a business to sell just a single product. Most will sell either a **product range** or a product mix. A business' product range is the different designs and specifications of a product that they sell, such as Coca-Cola's Zero, Light, Cherry and Caffeine-Free brands. The **product mix** is the mixture of different products a firm sells in different markets, such as Phillips power tools, irons and electric toothbrushes.

Exam style question 1

Jacinta Jones is an inventor who has invented a device designed to help parents locate children if they get lost. She has spent 3 years developing and testing the product and researching the market for parents of young children. She believes the technology could be adapted to retrieve lost property and find pets which have gone missing.

(a) Define the term 'product range'. *(2 marks)*

(b) Examine the benefits of Jacinta establishing a diverse product mix. *(4 marks)*

(c) Explain which stage of the product life cycle will earn least profits for Jacinta. *(4 marks)*

(d) Analyse two strategies Jacinta might use to prevent its product entering the decline stage of the product life cycle. *(4 marks)*

(e) There are similar products available, suggest ways in which Jacinta could differentiate her product from that of competitors. *(6 marks)*

Chapter review questions

1. Name the three parts of the design mix.
2. Give an example of a product that can be associated with each part of the design mix.
3. What are the stages of the product life cycle?
4. What is meant by an extension strategy?
5. Describe and give an example of the product range of a chosen business.
6. Describe and give an example of the product mix of a chosen business.
7. Why it is important for a business to differentiate their product?
8. How can a business differentiate its product from that of its competitors?

Key terms

The **aesthetics** of a product refers to the style of the product and how the design may attract a particular type of customer.

Differentiation of a product is when the product is given unique features to make it stand out from competitors. This may be done by branding or through product characteristics.

Extension strategies are adaptations made to a product, for example, new flavour of yogurt, used to prolong the maturity phase.

Function of a product is concerned with what the product is designed to do, how well it carries out this purpose and how long the product will last.

Product is the aspect of the marketing mix that refers to developing and providing a product that consumers want to buy.

The **product life-cycle** refers to the stages of life a product goes through from its introduction to its withdrawal from the market.

Product mix is the different types of product a business may produce, for example, Phillips produces a mix of products which include tools, irons and electric toothbrushes.

Product range is the different designs and specifications of a product, for example, Miele produces a range of vacuum cleaners.

Chapter 2.2.2

Price

Aims

By the end of this chapter, students should be able to understand:

- pricing strategies.
- influences on pricing strategies.

Pricing strategies

The pricing decision made by a business is often the key to the success and failure of the product. For example, a business such as an airline cannot just set a high price to seek high profit margins irrespective of market conditions. Such a strategy would likely lead to planes taking off with empty seats and low overall profit levels. If the same airline, however, tried to fill its planes by setting a low price irrespective of its costs of production, then it may find itself making a loss, which would be unsatisfactory for its shareholders.

The market forces of supply and demand determine price in many markets, such as stock markets, commodity markets and on online auction sites such as eBay. Where demand for a good is high but supply is low, such as property in busy cities like London or Birmingham, the many buyers bid up prices to a high level. If the supply of a product is higher than the numbers of potential buyers, then prices typically fall. This is why the cheapest time to buy Christmas cards is in January.

Businesses can use a range of different pricing strategies to sell their products. These include: cost-plus pricing, penetration pricing, competition pricing, skimming, and promotional pricing.

- **Cost-plus pricing** is where a business works out the average cost of production for its product and adds a percentage mark-up on top of the cost as profit. It can be a fairly simple way to set a price that ensures a profit is made on each sale. However, care must be taken to ensure that the price chosen is competitive within the market place.

Worked example of cost-plus pricing

Sparky's is a painting and decorating contractor that specialises in renovating houses and hotels. They give clients a price per room redecorated based on working out the average cost per room and then adding on 30% as profit.

Sparky's completed a renovation of a hotel in August 2017. The firm redecorated 150 rooms and spent a total of £26,000 on paint, brushes, wallpaper and labour. The price was calculated as:

Price charged = Average cost per room + Mark up

£26,000 / 150 rooms = £173.33 + 30% markup = £173.33 + (£173.33 x 0.3)

Final price per renovated room = £173.33 + £52.00 = **£225.33**

- **Penetration pricing** is where a low price is chosen to give a product a competitive edge in the market place. This strategy is often used to aid the introduction of a new product. Firms may even use **loss leader** pricing whereby they deliberately make a loss on a product in the short run in return for establishing a sizeable market share, or increasing sales of related products. There has been a lot of controversy about supermarkets in the UK using alcohol sales as loss leaders to attract customers to do their weekly shopping in their stores.
- **Competition pricing** is when a business prices the product according to what its competitors are charging for their product. This allows them to compete for market share on factors other than price. For example, Costa, Café Nero, and Starbucks all charge a similar price for a cup of coffee. They rarely compete on price, preferring to compete on content and non-price forms of promotion (such as customer loyalty schemes).

- **Skimming pricing** is a strategy whereby a firm sets a high price to maximise profits and recover some of the cost of researching and developing the product. This strategy tends to be associated with products that are new innovations in high demand and without competitors or viable substitutes. For example, Nike and Adidas sell their latest trainers at a higher price than their previous designs. Customers who are happy to buy last season's designs are able to buy the trainers at a lower price than when they were released. Skimming tends to be a short-run strategy because competitors are often quick to launch rival products to compete for market share. The latest Apple smartphone will be priced at a higher price than previous phones to give an impression of it having the latest technology and features.
- **Promotional pricing** is when a business temporarily reduces prices to attract extra customers. This might be used to clear excess stock when a product is being withdrawn or to give a new market segment a reason to try the product. Businesses hope to encourage repeat sales and brand loyalty through this strategy and thus increase the market share of their product in the long run. Clothing shops may have a summer sale, selling their clothes using an 'up to 50% off selected items' pricing strategy. This is attractive to customers who go in the shop to see what else is on offer (both discounted and full-price items).

Exam style question 1

Maguire's is a women's clothing label based in Dublin, Ireland. Its products are aimed at a professional market segment. Susan Maguire, the managing director of the company, creates a new range of winter wear each year. A coat from Maguire's costs £25 from its suppliers in India. After an initial opening day promotion offering 15% off the standard price to customers, Susan plans to sell the coats with a 500% mark-up.

(a) Define the term **cost-plus pricing**. *(2 marks)*

(b) What would be the selling price of a Maguire's coat after the opening day sale? *(2 marks)*

(c) Analyse the benefits of using promotional pricing. *(4 marks)*

(d) Examine whether Maguire's aims of profit maximisation might be better served through adopting a skimming pricing strategy when the product is launched. *(6 marks)*

Influences on pricing strategies

There are various factors which influence the pricing strategies used by businesses. These include: technology, competition, market segments and the product life cycle.

Technology – Technology may influence pricing strategies because innovative goods which are new to a market may use price skimming and charge a high price to attract *early adopters* (people who wish to be amongst the first people to own a new product). Higher prices are designed to give an impression of quality and high value added. Examples of price skimming include the latest model of iPad, drones, and laptops.

Price comparison websites, such as www.moneysupermarket.co.uk, have affected how businesses price their goods and services, as it is much easier for customers to compare prices of different goods and services.

Competition – Competitive markets have many firms selling similar products. Businesses which operate in competitive markets have to price their products so they are similar to their rivals. If they charge higher prices, customers will not tend to buy their products but if they lower their prices a price war may begin in which their competitors also lower prices. Examples of businesses which use competitive pricing include: hairdressers and cafés located in a small town, fresh food stalls in a market, and beauty salons offering services such as manicures and pedicures.

Market segments – Businesses produce goods and services aimed at different market segments. A person who plays a lot of golf as a hobby may be prepared to pay a high price for a set of golf clubs as compared to a person who plays a couple of rounds every year. A five-star hotel can charge high prices for its rooms as compared to a two-star hotel as they cater to different segments of the market.

Product life cycle – The stage in the life cycle of a product (see Chapter 2.2.1) will also influence the price of a product:

- **Introduction** – appropriate strategies include promotional pricing or penetration pricing (product operating in a competitive environment) or price skimming (for a new innovative product or a product aimed at higher income earners).
- **Growth** – if high prices were charged initially, they may start to fall as competition increases and more businesses join the market.
- **Maturity** – prices may be discounted to attract those customers who enjoy a bargain and are not concerned with switching to buy the latest version of a product.
- **Decline** – promotional pricing or loss leader pricing may be used to at least cover some costs of production. Goods such as digital cameras and DVD players can now be bought for very low prices as the demand for them has decreased.

Chapter review questions

1. Explain how prices are determined on auction websites such as eBay.
2. Explain the differences between skimming and penetration pricing.
3. If a product costs £3 to make but retails for £4, what is the profit mark-up?
4. Give three examples of products that are priced using competition pricing.
5. What are the main drawbacks of cost-plus pricing?
6. Describe how technology may influence pricing strategies.
7. Give two examples of how market segments may influence pricing strategies.
8. Give two examples of how competition may influence pricing strategies.
9. Give examples of how the stage in a product's life cycle may influence pricing strategies.

Key terms

Competition pricing is where a business prices a product according to what its competitors are charging for their product.

Cost-plus pricing is where a business works out the average cost of production of each unit of its product and adds a percentage mark-up on top as profit.

Loss leader occurs when a business charges a price for a product which is lower than the cost of producing the product, in order to increase market share or increase sales of related products.

Penetration pricing is where a low price is chosen to gain a product a competitive edge in the market place.

Promotional pricing is where a business temporarily reduces prices to attract extra customers.

Skimming pricing is a strategy whereby a firm sets a high price to maximise profits and recover some of the cost of researching and developing the product.

Chapter 2.2.3

Promotion

Aims

By the end of this chapter, students should be able to understand:

- appropriate promotion strategies for different market segments.
- the use of technology in promotion.

Appropriate promotion strategies for different market segments

Promotion can be defined as anything that a business does that is designed to increase awareness of, or boost sales of, their product or brand. Promotion can be categorised as either above-the-line or below-the-line.

Above-the-line promotion refers to any promotion that is placed in the media and paid for by the business. Primarily, when businesses refer to above-the-line promotion they are talking about advertising but there are other ways that businesses can pay to have their product highlighted in the media. Another increasingly popular above-the-line technique is **product placement** where a business pays to have their products used by certain movie or TV stars on screen. The James Bond franchise has numerous examples of this with the various sports cars and gadgetry used by the fictional secret agent. Large supermarkets and famous global brands such as fashion labels, cars and watches still use traditional forms of advertising, for example use of bill boards, TV advertising and advertising in magazines and newspapers. These may to appeal to mass markets although some brands such as high end fashion brands are aimed at high income earners who can afford the clothing.

Below-the-line promotion refers to any other type of promotion other than that of paid-for media. There are several methods used by businesses, including:

- Competitions – e.g. lucky draws, quizzes via email.
- Direct mail or email to consumers highlighting products and promotions.
- In-store point of sale displays.
- Loyalty card schemes in supermarkets e.g. Tesco's Club Card and Sainsbury's Nectar card encourage customers to stay loyal to the shop so they can collect points which can be redeemed for cash and other goods and services.
- Promotion via social media, e.g. Facebook, Instagram and SMS messages (see Chapter 1.4.3).

Advertising

Advertising is used by businesses to inform the consumer, persuade the consumer or a combination of both. **Persuasive advertising** is designed to encourage customers of rival businesses to switch brands and to give existing customers a reason to stay loyal to a brand or increase their consumption of it. Sounds and imagery are often used that appeal to a person's emotions, aspirations and fears. It will try to align the product with the values, tastes and interests of a particular market segment (see Chapter 1.2.3). A good example of persuasive advertising is L'Oréal's campaign for their shampoo. The beautiful people in the adverts convey an image of luxury and quality to the consumer. The 'because you're worth it' slogan encourages them to feel special enough to buy the product and in doing so, become as beautiful and happy as the celebrity or model endorsing the product in the advertisement.

Informative advertising tends to highlight the key aspects of a product rather than try to use advertising techniques that seek to persuade. For example, a football club will advertise details of the time, date and ticket prices for a forthcoming fixture. It is also typical to use informative advertising in a product's development stage to give consumers an awareness of the need or want the product is designed to satisfy.

Etihad is the major sponsor of Manchester City football team and their logo and brand name is placed on all football shirts worn by players.

Sponsorship

Businesses may pay to sponsor a famous sportsperson or an event in return for publicity of their support. Etihad is the major sponsor of Manchester City football team and their logo and brand name is placed on all football shirts worn by players. Local businesses sometimes sponsor local events, for example, summer fairs and school sports teams in return for publicity in school publications and their logo and name on the back of sports shirts. Other examples include, sponsoring a TV show or perhaps sponsorship of a sports star, such as Adidas' sponsorship of the athlete Jessica Ennis-Hill.

Product trials

Many Apps and software businesses offer free trials of their product as long as customers sign up and register by providing personal information. Spotify will allow customers to use its music streaming service for free but if customers want to listen to music offline they must subscribe to a premium service. A trial may be offered for a short period at a heavily discounted price. The customer must provide their bank account details to access the offer. People will often forget to cancel their subscription or find the service too attractive to give up and continue with their subscription. Gyms often offer a free trial to people and then use persuasive personal selling to persuade customers to join they gym and agree to a monthly subscription fee. Software manufactures also use a monthly subscription model to use their software. This ensures free updates but also allows the manufacturer to acquire data about what features of the software a person uses and to track their habits; in other words, access allows the business to collect free market research.

Special offers

- Businesses often use special offers to entice people to buy their goods and services. Examples include:
  - Free gifts, e.g. spend over £50 on Clinique cosmetics and receive a free travel set.
  - Free samples of new products e.g. cosmetic and personal grooming brands often give free samples of shampoo and moisturisers to customers.
  - Sales promotions such as buy-one-get-one-free often used by supermarkets.
  - Credit card companies which, e.g. offer a gift of rewards points to the first 10,000 customers who spend over a designated amount per month on their credit card.

Branding

Well-known brand names are a form of promotion. Agnes B is a fashion designer but her product range has extended to include a florist, café, restaurant and maker of chocolate and eye wear. The brand name is associated with high quality fashion and accessories and therefore people assume that the other products in the range are of the same high standard.

The use of technology in promotion

Technology is used widely as a means of promotion but by law businesses have to ask people to consent to receiving promotions, advertisements and marketing communications. This is usually done by signing a form in person or online. The Data Protection Act (1998) requires businesses to keep all personal information they have about customers private and they cannot share the information with other businesses or individuals.

- **Targeted advertising online**

  Many websites contain cookies which track our online browsing habits and retain this information. They store passwords and site preferences (the parts of the website you visit first). This information can be used by the business to create personalised advertisements for a customer based on their browsing habits.

  Google tracks the websites we visit and generates personalised advertising based on our searches. For example, a person who has researched flights to Greece may find advertisements for hotels and car hire in Greece appearing on web pages they are searching. Businesses such as Asos and www.zalora.com pay Google to advertise their websites to customers who have previously used their business when they are using the internet. Advertising is how Google makes a large portion of their income.

- **Viral advertising via social media**

  Instead of relying on advertisements to be aired on TV many businesses make advertisements which are uploaded straight to YouTube and successful advertisements are shared immediately via social media. Bloggers and vloggers are another means of promotion and some businesses will pay successful YouTube vloggers to promote their product on their channels. Social media is an increasingly important source of promotion as a huge proportion of the public accesses it using a hand held device. An example of a viral video is the annual John Lewis Christmas advert.

  Facebook is often used by small businesses because they can update their Facebook page immediately and do not have to keep updating webpages. This saves time, provides an instant means of communication, enables two-way communication with customers and is free!

- **E-Newsletters**

  Public and private sector organisations use e-newsletters (newsletters sent via email) to customers. Customers must have agreed to receive e-newsletters and they tend to be an informative form of advertising. For example, a theatre may send an e-newsletter informing patrons of up and coming shows and events. A local sports centre may send an e-newsletter with information about up and coming courses.

  The choice of media a business opts for is crucial. There is a wide variety of media that a business can choose to advertise their products. These include TV, radio, cinema, newspapers and magazines, billboards and the internet.

The choice of advertising media depends on a number of factors:

- The **marketing objectives** the business has. If the objective is to raise awareness of a brand then a billboard poster advert in a busy street might achieve this.
- The **target market** a business is aiming at is important as certain market segments may not view particular media in large numbers. For example, a business aiming at old age pensioners might not use internet advertising whereas a business aiming at teenagers would.
- The **coverage required** is a key consideration as a business looking for mass market appeal may naturally prefer mass media such as television.

- The **type of product** in question is important. If a sleek design is a key selling point for a product then radio advertising might not be a sensible choice as visual factors cannot be easily communicated.
- The marketing **budget** available might be the most important factor in choosing media. For a start-up business with little finance advertising on prime-time TV might not be an option given their budget constraint. They may instead look to cheaper alternatives such as a viral campaign on YouTube

Exam style questions

1. Outline a benefit of a business using social media to promote its products. *(3 marks)*
2. Justify which method of promotion would be suitable for a national chain of yoga studios, which offers a wide range of classes throughout the week and also lessons in workplaces and clients' homes:

   (a) E-newsletter to clients.

   (b) Celebrity endorsement using posters on billboards. *(9 marks)*

Chapter review questions

1. Explain the difference between persuasive and informative advertising.
2. Name two types of business that may use sponsorship as a means of promotion.
3. Give two advantages of a product trial.
4. State two disadvantages of using special offers as a means of promotion.
5. Explain the advantages a branded product may have over a non-branded product.
6. Explain two advantages and two disadvantages of targeted advertising online.
7. Discuss advantages and disadvantages of viral advertising on social media.
8. Explain reasons why a business may use an e-newsletter to promote their products and services.

Key terms

Above-the-line promotion refers to any promotion that is placed in the media and paid for by the business.

Below-the-line promotion refers to any other type of promotion other than paid-for media.

E-newsletters are newsletters containing information about a business's products sent by email to customers.

Informative advertising tends to highlight the key aspects of a product rather than try to use advertising techniques that seek to persuade.

Persuasive advertising is designed to encourage people to buy a product instead of that of a rivals' and maintain the custom of existing customers.

Product placement occurs when a business pays to have its products used in a film or by TV stars on screen.

Promotion refers to the strategies a business can use to inform consumers about its products or services and persuade them to make a purchase.

Social media are digital communication platforms which include: Facebook, Instagram and Twitter.

Chapter 2.2.4

Place

Aims

By the end of this chapter, students should be able to understand:

- methods of distribution: retailers and e-tailers (e-commerce).

Methods of distribution

The 'place' aspect of the marketing mix refers to how and where the consumer is able to purchase the product. The manner in which the product gets to the final consumer can be a key competitive edge for a business. For a frozen food manufacturer, it is essential that their products are carried by retailers like supermarket chains to ensure high sales volumes. The airline Easyjet was one of the pioneers of selling flights on-line and is therefore an e-tailer. Consumers quickly took to this convenient method of booking flights, and costs for Easyjet were lower than their competitors who still relied on travel agents to process bookings. This helped the business to keep prices low and establish a sizeable market share.

The **channel of distribution** refers to the number of intermediaries that a product goes through after production until it reaches the final consumer. A typical distribution channel is shown in Figure 2.2.4

Figure 2.2.4a: Typical distribution channel

The length of the distribution channel will depend on the type of product and the objectives of the business. Using a wholesaler and then retailers allows a large company like Kellogg's to focus on making and marketing the product and allowing the businesses further along in the supply chain to share some of the costs of storage and distribution. It also allows Kellogg's to take advantage of trading economies of scale as they cut down on administrative costs incurred in the sale process through dealing with fewer customers that place very large orders. The wholesaler, in turn, will sell the product on in smaller quantities to retailers, which act as a 'breaker of bulk' and sells the cereal individually to the consumer, who benefits from not having to purchase large quantities at a time.

Businesses can use one of, or a combination of, the following methods to distribute their product to the customer.

Retailers

Retailers are businesses which sell goods and services directly to the public. Examples include:

- Department stores such as John Lewis and Selfridges sell the products of a wide variety of businesses in their store. For example, their electronics section will sell the products of Sony and Samsung.
- Chain stores such as Apple stores are established by businesses as a platform to sell their goods without going via an intermediary.
- Discount stores are stores which buy up large quantities of branded goods, such as out-of-season-clothing and sell them at a discounted price.
- Superstores are large stores such as Wal-Mart where consumers can buy a wide variety of goods from computers to kitchen utensils.
- Supermarkets primarily sell groceries but also sell a wide variety of goods such as kitchenware, clothes and gardening equipment.
- Small independent shops which sell goods straight to the customer.

Advantages of retailers

- Customers can see, sample and try on the product.
- Customers receive personal customer service and get immediate answers to questions about the product.
- Displays and personal selling may entice customers to purchase more products than they originally intended.

Disadvantages of retailers

- Renting or buying premises for the shops is costly.
- High running costs may mean that they have to charge higher prices to cover costs.

Direct sales

- Direct sales involve the producer selling directly to the consumer. Dell, for example, sells computers directly to the customer. Some insurance businesses sell policies over the phone. A person selling homemade cushions and quilts on a market stall sells directly to the customer.
- Mail order selling is becoming less and less frequent as the internet becomes a more popular way of buying products. However, some firms still earn high revenues through sending out a catalogue of products, taking orders by post and then delivering the goods to the consumer. Argos still operates a system whereby customers choose goods from a physical catalogue in store or an online catalogue. They order and pay for the goods at a counter and then wait for the goods to be retrieved from a store room behind the counter. Not having the goods on display reduces cost of display space and therefore overall costs of the goods sold.

E-tailers (e-commerce)

- E-commerce has become as important in some markets as shopping in a retail outlet. This is particularly noticeable in the entertainment market where Amazon, iTunes and Netflix have made shopping online, listening to music and watching films, more interactive and convenient.
- Many retailers also have a website as well as a retail outlet from which customers can buy products. Supermarkets allow shopping over the internet with home delivery and department stores such as John Lewis are both retailers and e-tailers.
- Shopping online has become increasingly popular. Websites such as ASOS allows people to purchase clothes and footwear online and it offers free delivery worldwide on orders over £8.27 and free returns.
- Businesses such as Amazon and eBay sell a vast number of goods over the internet and are hugely popular and successful.

Advantages of e-tailers

- Customers can purchase goods 24/7.
- E-tailers can access a global market because they sell over the internet.
- Lack of physical shops means that running costs are lower and therefore the e-tailer may be able to lower prices.

Disadvantages of e-tailers

- Customers cannot try and test the product
- Although fixed costs may be lower, the costs of transporting goods to customers are higher.
- Customers may have to pay to return or exchange goods and this may deter them from buying goods online.
- If an e-tailer allows free returns and exchange this will increase costs.

Exam style question

Kasey Parisa Ltd. has designed a new brand of dairy and gluten free ice cream. Retail customers are able to purchase the ice cream in batches of 20 cartons using the company's website. Kasey Parisa is the proprietor. She is looking to explore alternative distribution channels.

(a) Define the term 'channel of distribution'. *(2 marks)*

(b) What is the main disadvantage of being an e-tailer and selling the product exclusively via the website? *(4 marks)*

(c) Evaluate the impact to Kasey Parisa Ltd. of using retail customers (such as supermarkets) to sell its products. *(6 marks)*

Advantages and disadvantages of using different distribution channels

Method of distribution	Advantages	Disadvantages
Wholesalers	• Allow large producers to supply small businesses through their breaking of bulk. • Supply goods to smaller retailers on credit. • Take on some of the storage and distribution costs for both the producer and the smaller retailer.	• Take a share of profits. • Do not have a good picture of consumer needs and wants so may be slow to react to market changes.
Superstore/ Supermarket/ Department store	• Knowledge of local markets. • Place large orders. • May be skilled in marketing and promotional activity.	• They will add a mark-up to the price which may make the producer's product uncompetitive. • They might market products in a way the producer does not like.
Chain store	• A company like Apple has more control of the marketing and promotions of its products when sold at its own stores. • Sales assistants are likely to be more knowledgeable, e.g. staff should know more about Sony products in a Sony store than in an electrical wholesaler. • Profit stays within the company and is not passed on to a third-party retailer, e.g. if Apple sells via its own chain stores they do not need to share profits with other wholesalers or retailers.	• High overheads may be incurred to maintain a town centre presence. • Consumers may prefer to shop in stores with a greater variety of products than in a chain store offering only one brand.
Small shops	• Often stock goods unavailable in larger shops. • May provide personalised service.	• Prices may be higher than in larger stores.
Direct selling	• Agents can build relationships with customers, and may have well-developed sales skills and knowledge of the local market.	• Sales agents for the business need to be paid and take a commission. • Agents that are too persistent or use unethical tactics can damage the business' brand.
Mail order	• Businesses may allow customers the flexibility of paying for goods in instalments and on credit. • Convenient for consumers who find it difficult to go shopping.	• It is not convenient to sell some goods via mail order. • Problems with delivery can damage the reputation of the business.
E-tailers (e-commerce – selling on the internet)	• Customers can learn more about the product through reading reviews. • Simple, quick and convenient for consumers who can shop 24 hours a day. • Can reduce business overheads such as rent on retail space.	• Some market segments may not typically purchase on the internet. • Some consumers may want the help and advice of a shop assistant. • Delivery costs of getting goods to customers increases.

Chapter review questions

1. Describe two advantages of using a wholesaler.
2. Explain and give an example of direct selling.
3. What are two advantages and disadvantages of selling on the internet?
4. Identify five examples of retailer.
5. Explain two advantages and disadvantages of selling goods in a department store.
6. Identify and explain two advantages of being an e-tailer.
7. Identify and explain two disadvantages of being an e-tailer.

Key terms

The **channel of distribution** refers to the number of intermediaries that a product goes through after production until it reaches the final consumer.

E-tailers are businesses that sell goods to customers over the internet.

Place refers to the method or methods a business uses to get its product to the consumer.

Retailers are businesses that sells goods to the general public (customers).

Wholesaler acts as a 'breaker of bulk' by buying large quantities of goods from manufacturers and selling goods in smaller quantities to retailers.

Chapter 2.2.5

Using the marketing mix to make business decisions

Aims

By the end of this chapter, students should be able to understand:

- how each element of the marketing mix can influence other elements.
- how the marketing mix can build competitive advantage.
- how an integrated marketing mix can influence competitive advantage.

How each element of the marketing mix can influence other elements?

Each element of the marketing mix can influence other elements. For example:

High **prices** may give an impression that the product is of high quality and equally low prices may suggest product of low quality.

- Expensive goods such as a Dior or Chanel handbag are associated with high quality and the brand name adds value (see Chapter 1.1.3) to the product. The brand name itself is a form of **promotion**.
- Celebrity endorsement may promote the product, increase its popularity and may give an impression of high quality product. Examples include:
  - Heston Blumenthal's range of eyewear for Vision Express increased their sales (promotion and product).
  - Jamie Oliver's advertising campaign for Sainsbury's was expensive but created profits for the supermarket (product and promotion).
  - Many fashion brands use celebrities such as Cristiano Ronaldo, Shaquille O'Neal, Hailey Baldwin, Kendall Jenner, to post pictures on Instagram and Twitter of them wearing their clothes and accessories (promotion and product).
- Special or limited editions may be charged at a higher price.
  - For example, Adidas puts 'Special Edition' on new lines of trainers to give the impression there is something unusual or selective about the line of trainers which may entice customers to buy them.
  - KitKat has created limited edition flavours of their famous chocolate bar giving the impression the limited edition bar will only be available for a short time period.
- Innovative products may charge a higher price for their products and sell a limited number.
  - Apple uses price skimming for new products which tend to be product oriented (see Chapter 2.2.1) and makes them available in a limited number of shops and in limited numbers online when first released (price and place).

Using the marketing mix to build competitive advantage

A business may use the marketing mix to build a competitive advantage. For example, Sports Direct has the following marketing mix focused mainly on a wide range of discounted products and has built competitive advantage on its low price low frills approach:

Product – Sports Direct sells a wide product range of sportswear, sports equipment, casual clothing and accessories. It has a low cost "pile 'em high, sell 'em cheap" strategy where goods are stored in the shop instead of in a stock room to maximise use of the retail space. Sports Direct sells a large number of well-known brands at discounted prices.

Price – tries to be as low as possible to undercut competitors. Customer service (see Chapter 2.3.4) tends to be poor and costs are minimised through a small number of shop assistants and low expenditure on in-store displays.

Promotion – Sports Direct has received a large amount of negative publicity due to the number of staff employed on zero hours contracts and a reputation for substandard customer service. Despite the negative publicity a large number of customers will take advantage of the cheaper prices. Other customers will however shop elsewhere.

Place – it sells in retail shops and online and customers can shop 24/7. Sports Direct will ship goods overseas and therefore reaches an extensive market.

How an integrated marketing mix can influence competitive advantage

An integrated marketing mix can influence competitive advantage. For example Waitrose the supermarket has the following marketing mix which has allowed it to attract customers in areas where it is located:

Product – high quality food and household products. It also has an 'essential range' of basic food products with lower prices. Waitrose sells its own products as well as those of other manufacturers

Price – premium pricing to create a corporate image of Waitrose selling high quality products.

Promotion – Examples of below-the-line promotion (see Chapter 2.2.3) include the Waitrose loyalty scheme called myWaitrose. This provides customers with free coffee or tea when shopping in the store and provides other offers such as 20% off fish on Fridays, discounted dry cleaning and a free cookery magazine and to encourage customer loyalty. Its above-the-line advertising (see Chapter 2.2.3) includes, television adverts and videos promoting the freshness of its foods. For example, it shot a video of Heston Blumenthal on a fishing boat in the North Sea where Waitrose sources its sustainably caught fish.

Place – Most Waitrose stores are located in the South East of England with fewer branches in other parts of the country. Goods can be bought online as well as in store. Waitrose sells products in Hong Kong supermarkets where even the essential range is perceived to be a product from a premium British supermarket and as an imported product achieves higher prices than if sold in Britain.

The combination of high quality products, a personalised Waitrose App and free drinks whilst shopping has influenced its competitive advantage and helps to retain loyal customers.

Waitrose uses premium pricing to create a corporate image of selling high quality products.

Exam style question 1

Waterstones offers shoppers a retail experience in their book shops because in addition to their product range of books, cards, stationery and other gifts staff offer advice on books and write book reviews. There is a café, a children's section, where children are encouraged to read books and play with toys, and book readings and signing events regularly take place. There are toilets and changing facilities for babies. Customers pay a slightly higher price for products than if they were bought online as customers can visit the shops, handle the books, read excerpts and do so whilst enjoying a cup of coffee if they wish to.

In October 2014 a customer got locked in the Trafalgar Waterstones branch when the shop closed and tweeted that he was locked in. There was an unbelievably positive response from many Twitter users and Waterstones shoppers to the American customer being able to spend time amongst books. Airbnb cheekily tweeted about Waterstones turning into an Airbnb host and this spawned an idea for creating publicity for the book shop and for Airbnb. Both businesses created a competition asking customers to say in one sentence which book they would read and why if they had a sleepover in Waterstones and why to decide who could have a sleepover in the store. Ten pairs of tickets were distributed and the sleepover took place. For minimal financial expenditure Waterstones and Airbnb gained a lot of positive publicity

Question

1. Evaluate how the integrated marketing mix of Waterstones influenced competitive advantage. *(12 marks)*

Chapter review questions

1. Give an example of how each element of the marketing mix of business can influence other elements.
2. Explain how the marketing mix can help to build competitive advantage.
3. Explain how an integrated marketing mix can influence competitive advantage.

Key terms

Competitive advantage is the advantage a business may have over its competitor's e.g. lower prices or unique products or service.

Marketing mix refers to the components of an effective marketing strategy. The mix consists of product, price, promotion and place.

Chapter 2.3.1

Business operations

Aims

By the end of this chapter, students should be able to understand:

- the purpose of business operations.
- production processes.
- the impact of different types of production process.
- the impacts of technology on production.

The purpose of business operations

The purpose of business operations includes:

- to produce goods, e.g. clothing, shoes, bread, cars, computers, smartphones and jewellery.
- to produce services, e.g. hairdresser, restaurants, healthcare providers, hotels, martial arts studios, and child minding.

Production processes

Production is the process which changes raw materials into finished goods and services. There are three main methods of production: job production, batch production, and flow production.

Job production

Job production refers to production of unique or one-of-a-kind goods. The individual item is made from start to finish and requires a high level of skill and expertise to complete the process. It is therefore a labour-intensive production process.

Examples of goods and services made using job production include: made-to-measure (custom-made) suit or dress, made-to-order wedding or birthday cake, made-to-order furniture, construction of bridges, tunnels and aircraft, a haircut, the interior design of a house and a taxi journey.

Advantages of job production	Disadvantages of job production
A high quality product is usually produced.	Production process is time consuming and therefore costs may be high.
Product can be customised precisely to meet the needs of the customer.	Highly skilled workers are expensive and may be difficult to find.
Workers are highly skilled and the work tends not to be repetitive; this can lead to personal satisfaction and a motivated workforce.	The business may be small in size and therefore unable to take advantage of economies of scale.

Batch production

Batch production is when goods or parts of goods are made in groups or batches, e.g. in a bakery the ingredients for bread will be mixed and then left to rise before baking. Components (parts) of goods are often made in batches, e.g. a clothing manufacturer may divide the task into parts: cutting, sewing and finishing. Batches of the semi-finished garments may be stored until they are required.

Many businesses produce goods that are broadly similar but vary slightly in design, e.g. shampoo to suit different hair types. The business will make a number of items (a batch) of one type of product and then change to the production of a different type of product. Most manufactured goods are made using batch production, e.g. a jam producer will make a batch of strawberry jam, followed by a batch of blackcurrant jam.

Batch production is common because it allows a degree of customisation. This means that clothes can be made in different sizes, colours and designs. Examples of goods and services made using batch production include: bottled drinks, lipstick, bread, components for electronic goods, coloured pencils and package holidays.

Advantages of batch production	Disadvantages of batch production
The production process is faster than job production and therefore the cost per unit is lower so it may be possible to take advantage of economies of scale.	Time is wasted between the production of different batches as the machinery and equipment needs to be cleaned and reorganised.
It allows a degree of customisation e.g. different types of bread, designs of t-shirts, colours of lipstick.	Storage of semi-finished and finished goods requires space and this increases cost. There is also a risk that goods may get damaged or never be used.
Workers are more specialised and the production process becomes more automated and this can reduce costs per unit.	As workers become more specialised they may become bored, which can affect motivation.

Flow production

Continuous flow production occurs when identical products are made on a production line. Chicken nuggets are an example of goods made using flow production; live chickens are slaughtered at the beginning of the production line and frozen chicken nuggets are the end product. The process is highly mechanised and machinery carries the chicken in its various stages of processing through the factory. Car manufacturing is another example of flow production. Flow production is capital-intensive which means there is a higher ratio of machines to humans in the production process.

Other examples of goods and services made using flow production include: Coca–Cola in bottles and cans, mass produced crisps, mass produced biscuits, breakfast cereal and oil refining.

Advantages of flow production	Disadvantages of flow production
Identical products are produced efficiently and quickly and therefore costs per unit are lower and the firm can take advantage of economies of scale.	The machinery tends to be highly inflexible and therefore it is difficult to change the design of the products or produce a different product.
The production process is highly mechanised and this reduces labour costs.	The cost of the machinery and capital equipment is very high.
The machinery can operate 24 hours per day.	Flow production is capital-intensive and workers' may be very specialised; they may become bored, which can affect motivation.
Modern technology can allow mass-customisation of some goods, e.g. cars (customers can order a standard car and personalise it by choosing from a range of colours and features).	A breakdown of the machinery will bring production to a stop.

Use and management of resources in job, batch and flow production

Method of production	Human resources	Capital resources	Productivity = output per worker
Job	Highly skilled workers	More labour-intensive	Low
Batch	Skilled workers/ less skilled workers	More even distribution of labour and capital resources	Greater output per worker
Flow	Low skilled workers	Capital-intensive	High (there tends to be fewer workers)

Exam style question 1

(a) Vortex Cinema is an independent film house that shows old and new films. It produces a monthly brochure of forthcoming films which it distributes in schools, restaurants, bars and cafes in the local area. Explain two reasons why Vortex Cinema will produce its brochures using batch production. *(4 marks)*

(b) Jacksons Garment Ltd. is a company that designs wedding dresses which are produced on a large scale in China for sale in department stores and wedding dress shops throughout the UK. Fiona Clark designs and makes wedding dresses for individual customers. Justify which type of production method should be used in each business and explain your answer in each case. *(4 marks)*

The impact of different types of production process

Productivity measures how efficiently factors of production are used to generate output. It is calculated by comparing the output to the factor input:

$$\textbf{Productivity} = \frac{\textbf{Output}}{\textbf{Input}}$$

For example, **labour productivity** can be measured by the output per worker. Consider the numerical examples below as a point of illustration (assume both firms operate in the same industry):

	Firm A	Firm B
Output (units)	20,000	15,000
Workers	500	300
Productivity	20,000 / 500 = 400 units per worker	15,000 / 300 = 500 units per worker

Hence, it can be seen that whilst Firm A produces more output in absolute terms, Firm B is more efficient as the average worker produces an extra 100 units compared to its rival business.

Labour input can also be expressed as the hours worked, i.e. output per hour. The increased number of businesses that employ staff on a part-time or temporary basis suggests that measuring labour productivity by labour hours is more accurate as a measure of labour productivity. Another method that suits some businesses is to measure the sales revenue per worker:

	Firm A	Firm B
Sales revenue	£1,000,000	£900,000
Workers	200	300
Productivity	£1,000,000 / 200 = £5,000 per worker	£900,000 / 300 = £3,000 per worker

An alternative measure of productivity is to look at **capital productivity**. Here the output is compared to the capital input, e.g. number of machines, of a business. For example:

	Firm A	Firm B
Output (units)	15,000	12,000
Capital (number of machines)	5	4
Productivity	15,000 / 5 = 3,000 units per machine	12,000 / 4 = 3,000 units per machine

The main benefit of higher productivity for a business is the efficiency gains – there is increased output per unit of factor input. This means that the factors of production are being used more effectively, possibly giving the business a cost advantage. This will subsequently lead to higher profits.

Job production tends to be the most expensive type of production process as it requires skilled workers and products tend to be made-to-order. The production process may take a long time and therefore costs and prices will be higher than similar products produced in larger quantities. Customers are paying more for the skilled labour and individualised product.

Batch production is the most common type of production because it enables a degree of flexibility and different sizes, flavours and styles of product can be made. Products are made in greater number and therefore productivity increases and unit costs fall. Batch production allows a larger number of products to be made and prices should be more competitive. McDonald's has changed to allow customers to customise their burgers to an extent.

Flow production produces identical products and requires fewer workers and more machinery. Productivity is high as machines can operate 24 hours a day if necessary. Unit costs will be lower and prices tend to be very competitive. Firms which are dominant in the industry may be price leaders (this means they charge a low price and cause other firms to follow their lead and drop prices).

Impacts of technology on production

Technology continues to revolutionise production with the increase in use of 3D printing and software to produce goods and services. 3D printers are expensive and require a substantial amount of initial capital investment but they minimise wasted materials and allow for customisation of products for customers and therefore enable **flexibility**. 3D printing may eventually enable firms to produce goods more quickly and cheaply and allow new competitors into markets.

People no longer need a travel agent to arrange holidays as they can do it alone online and often consult websites such as https://en.tripadvisor.com.hk and www.booking.com to assist with choices.

Technology can also be used by a tailor making a suit for a regular customer. Their measurements and previous orders are stored and software can be used to cut out patterns and ensure minimum waste of material thus increasing **productivity**. Technology may also enable a better **quality** of product to be produced as automated processes will allow for less mistakes and defects. Many will argue that technology cannot always replicate the detail and expertise of hand sewing. High end fashion labels such as Armani still employ professional embroiderers to hand stitch designs onto garments.

Traditional production lines tend to have dedicated machinery and those businesses that adopt new technologies may find themselves ahead of those who continue with the traditional practices. It is important, however, to balance **cost** of technology with pricing strategies and overall cost of production to ensure a business's survival. Technology may also enable a better quality of product to be produced and automated processes will allow for less mistakes and defects and there will be greater flexibility in the production process.

Exam style question 2

3D Models is an established business which builds models of buildings for architectural practices. Until recently they have been creating 3D models by hand and each model is made to order for a client. They have purchased a 3D printer which prints the model. This has revolutionised the way in which the business operates. Current employees need training to use the software which accompanies the printer.

Questions

(a) Outline one impact on 3D Models of using a 3D printer to print the model instead of building by hand. *(2 marks)*

(b) Analyse the purchase of the 3D printer in terms of cost, productivity, flexibility and quality. *(9 marks)*

Chapter review questions

1. Explain three characteristics of each method of production (job, batch and flow).
2. Outline two advantages and two disadvantages of each method of production (job, batch and flow).
3. Give two reasons why workers need to be very skilled to perform job production.
4. Explain why batch production is the most common form of production method.
5. Explain why flow production requires a high ratio of capital equipment.
6. Explain which type of production creates the most competitive prices.
7. Explain the impact of technology on production in terms of balancing cost, productivity, quality and flexibility.

Key terms

Batch production occurs when goods or parts of goods are made in groups or batches, e.g. in a bakery the ingredients for bread will be mixed and then left to rise before baking.

Flow production occurs when identical products are made on a continuous production line.

Job production refers to production of unique or one-of-a-kind goods. The individual item is made from start to finish and requires a high level of skill and expertise to complete the process.

Productivity measures how efficiently factors of production are used to generate output. It is calculated by comparing the output to the factor input (often number of workers).

Chapter 2.3.2

Working with suppliers

Aims

By the end of this chapter, students should be able to understand:

- stock management.
- the use of just in time (JIT) stock control.
- the role of procurement.
- the impact of logistics and supply decisions.

Stock management

Managing stock is very important in a business for the following reasons:

- Stocks are an essential part of the production process and delays in receiving stock may delay the production process.
- Supplies of stock need to be stored and storage adds to business costs.
- Stocks may become obsolete or damaged whilst being stored.
- Money spent on stock could be spent elsewhere in the business.

Just-in-time (**JIT**) is a lean stock control system used to eliminate the costs of holding stock. There are three main types of stock that a business might have:

- Raw materials – these are factors of production from the primary industry.
- Work-in-progress – these are semi-finished goods or components, e.g. an unsprayed car.
- Finished goods – these goods are ready to be sold to the customer, e.g. a fully manufactured car.

Traditional stock control systems require businesses to hold a certain minimum level of stock (known as the **buffer stock**) just in case there is a need for them. However, this can be inefficient and costly (see table below). By contrast, JIT relies on the use of computerised stock control systems to allow a business to operate without a buffer stock. Instead, stocks are delivered as and when they are needed for production, i.e. just in time. For JIT to work, the business must have a good working relationship with its suppliers to ensure that goods arrive on time and are of good quality. Aldi is an example of a business that uses a JIT system of stock control. This helps Aldi to cut costs associated with holding too much stock which include: warehouse space, staff to manage warehouse, risk of stock getting damaged or going out of date.

Advantages of holding stock	Disadvantages of holding stock
Prevents any potential delays in output as there are sufficient stocks for production.	Storage costs – this might include maintenance and security costs in some cases.
Having stocks means the business can meet its orders on time and increase its sales revenue.	Opportunity cost – the money used to buy, store and maintain stocks might have been used more efficiently elsewhere.
Timely output and availability of goods can enhance customer satisfaction and boost the firm's reputation.	Increased wastage – this might be caused by stocks being damaged, stolen or out-dated (perishable products and obsolete products).
	Collectively, this means that holding high levels of stock damages a firm's cash flow (see Chapter 1.3.3).

A traditional stock control system that is dependent on holding a minimum stock level (see Figure 2.3.2a) has several important features as shown in the bar gate stock graph.

- *Maximum stock level* – the highest volume of stock that a business is willing or able to hold at any point in time.
- *Re-order stock level* – the stock level at which the business places a new order from its supplier.
- *Minimum stock level* – the buffer stock, i.e. the lowest level of stock that the business is prepared to hold just in case of supplier or production delays.
- *Re-order amount* – the quantity of stock that a business orders from its supplier.
- *Lead time* – the time lag (delay) between placing an order and receiving the stock.

Figure 2.3.2a: Bar gate stock graph of a traditional (just-in-case) stock control system

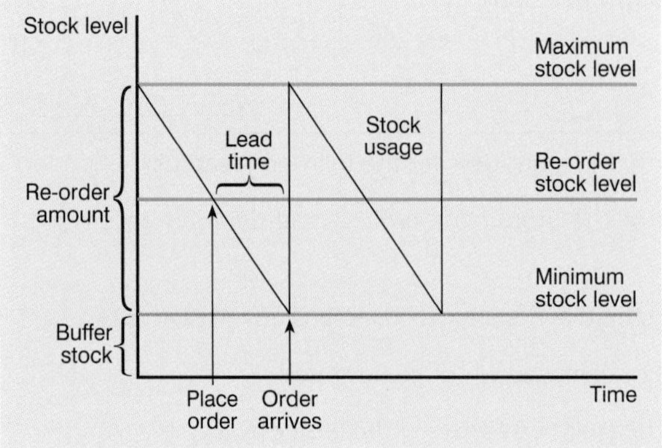

Advantages of JIT	Disadvantages of JIT
Improved cash flow as there is no need to hold buffer stocks, with their associated costs.	If the supplier is delayed, the business does not have any buffer stocks to continue with production.
Less wastage as stocks are less prone to theft, damage or becoming obsolete.	Similarly, JIT systems rely on external organisations to be efficient, which is beyond the firm's control.
JIT allows businesses to be more responsive to changes in demand.	JIT increases the frequency of stock orders, thereby raising administrative costs

Figure 2.3.2b illustrates a JIT stock control system. In a JIT system:

- Orders tend to take place more frequently than in a traditional system.
- No buffer stock is held.
- When the reorder level of stock is reached a message is automatically sent to suppliers who arrange an order of stock to be delivered.
- The supplier guarantees that stock will arrive in an agreed amount of time after receipt of order.
- Lead time is constant.

Figure 2.3.2b: Bar gate stock graph of a just-in-time stock control system

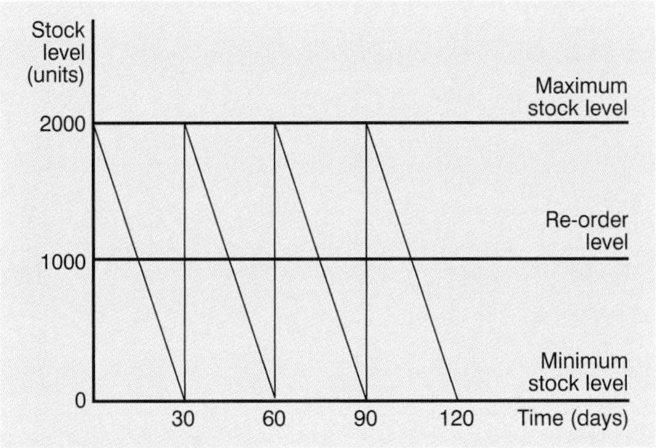

Exam style question

Study Figure 2.3.2b above and answer the following questions:

1. Identify the reorder level of stock. *(1 mark)*
2. Calculate the lead time. *(1 mark)*
3. Calculate how much stock is in each order. *(1 mark)*
4. Analyse the cost and benefits of a just-in-time stock control system over a traditional stock control system. *(6 marks)*

The role of procurement: Relationship with suppliers

Procurement is the act of buying goods and services. For a JIT stock control system to work a business needs to have a **strong relationship** with its suppliers to ensure that when a re-order for stock is placed the suppliers get the stock to the business before their existing stock runs out, in other words just-in-time. The supplier must **guarantee** that after an order for stock is placed it is delivered within an agreed amount of time as any delays in the process will prevent the business fulfilling its own orders.

JIT suppliers must:

- Supply stocks of consistent **quality** with no defects.
- Guarantee delivery **speed** and **reliability** at affordable **cost**.
- Ensure stocks are always **available**.
- Create complete **trust** between the business and the supplier.

The stock supplied must also be of **good quality** without any defects. If there are imperfections the stock will be unusable and the production process may be interrupted. Large manufacturing organisations tend to have a computerised stock management system which will automatically send an order of stock to suppliers when stock reaches a particular level.

The impact of logistics and supply decisions on costs, reputation and customer satisfaction

Overall costs should decrease after implementation of a JIT system as although administration costs may increase for a business because more orders for stock are made this increase should be cancelled out by **decreases in storage costs and costs** caused by faulty supplies.

The **reputation** of the business may improve because JIT should lead to greater **customer satisfaction** because of fewer defective finished products and the business may become a JIT supplier to their customers.

Chapter review questions

1. Explain why it is important to manage the level of stock held in a business.
2. Describe how a traditional stock management system works.
3. Explain the characteristics of a JIT stock management system.
4. Describe the relationship a business must have with its supplier for a JIT system to work.
5. Explain the impact of JIT on costs, reputation and consumer satisfaction.

Key terms

Buffer stock is a minimum amount of stock a business will hold in a traditional stock management system.

Customer satisfaction refers to how happy the customer is with the quality of service received.

Just-In-Time (JIT) is a lean stock control system which relies on having stocks (of raw materials, components and finished products) delivered timely to eliminate the costs of holding buffer stocks.

Lead time is the time lag (delay) between placing an order and receiving the stock.

Lean production is a production philosophy that strives to reduce or eliminate waste (time, effort and resources) in the activities of a business.

Procurement is the act of buying goods and services.

Productivity measures how well factors of production (such as labour or capital) are used to generate output. It is calculated by comparing the output to the factor input, e.g. output per worker.

Chapter 2.3.3

Managing quality

Aims

By the end of this chapter, students should be able to understand:

- The concept of quality and its importance.
- Quality control and quality assurance.
- Learning outcome: importance of quality to control costs and gain a competitive advantage.

The concept of quality and its importance in the production of goods and the provision of services

Quality is vitally important to any business interested in building a successful brand, attracting new customers and keeping existing customers loyal to the product. Quality might mean different things in different contexts. Easyjet flies passengers to destinations in planes without business or first class seats and food is not provided free of charge. This contrasts with British Airways flights but nevertheless Easyjet might still be proud of the quality of its service because it delivered to the customer exactly what was paid for and expected.

Managers in most companies are constantly focusing on maintaining existing standards and improving quality where possible. A failure to provide quality can have a hugely negative impact on businesses, for example:

- Customers may switch to other brands.
- Customers may share their opinions on the shortcomings of a business' product with others. This can be disastrous for both sales and profits.
- Defective products must be corrected and, sometimes, compensation given.

Quality control and quality assurance

- The **traditional quality control** method is to take a sample of the end product of a business and check that it meets the required standards. This might be testing manufactured products at the end of a production line, food in a restaurant, or sending a 'mystery shopper' into a retail outlet. Checking quality in this manner may identify a problem in the production process and prevent faulty goods reaching the consumer. However, this method would not give the business much information in terms of identifying the source of the problem or finding solutions in order to eradicate it. In addition, many businesses would employ staff to carry out quality control checks and register defects but not readily identify solutions.
- **Quality assurance** is where the business builds quality control into every single stage and aspect of production rather than checking for quality at the end. It makes quality the job of a few individuals or a department. This means that quality becomes part of every employee's job description and the responsibility of everyone from the office intern right up to the CEO. Quality assurance is also seen as an ongoing process and businesses continually seek improvements to it.
- **Total quality management (TQM)** is a system of promoting and checking quality at every stage of the production process. This approach requires all employees taking responsibility for assuring quality.

Advantages and disadvantages of quality assurance

Advantages	Disadvantages
Quality is built in to every aspect of the business and becomes central to the ethos.	Adding responsibilities to employee's roles can lead to resistance.
The business works to eliminate defects completely by adopting a 'right first time' approach.	Training might be needed to aid implementation of the process, which can be costly.
Waste is reduced and efficiency improves. The businesses can expect increased sales based on an enhanced product image.	

Exam style question 1

Bare Fit is a private members gym in Newcastle. It has 500 paying members. Recently the customer relations manager responsible for quality has received a lot of negative feedback from customers about the poor customer service of the personal trainers and the aggressive attitude of the sales staff. In the past, complaints have been made about the food on sale in the café.

(a) Assess the importance of promoting quality in the health and fitness industry. *(4 marks)*

(b) Analyse the costs and benefits of the traditional approach to quality currently employed by Bare Fit. *(4 marks)*

(c) Justify whether Bare Fit should change to a TQM system to improve quality. *(9 marks)*

Cost control and competitive advantage

A business which produces quality goods and provides quality services is likely to have a strong reputation in their field for selling high-quality goods which may give them an advantage over their competitors. When buying a kitchen appliance customers may choose brands such as Hotpoint, Hoover, Zanussi, and Miele over unknown brands.

Effective quality assurance will also help to control costs and may even reduce costs. Reasons include:

- Less defects means less wasted materials.
- Fewer goods returned by customers which will lower administration and replacement costs.
- Making all workers responsible for the quality process may improvement motivation levels (see Chapter 2.5.4) which leads to efficient production and lower costs.

Chapter review questions

1. Explain why a Volkswagen and a Ferrari can both claim to be a quality product.
2. Give 3 reasons why a business should strive for quality.
3. Explain the traditional method of quality control.
4. Highlight the key drawbacks of traditional quality control.
5. Define quality assurance.
6. List the advantages of quality assurance.
7. List the disadvantages of quality assurance.
8. Explain how quality assurance can control costs.
9. Explain how quality assurance can help a business gain a competitive advantage.

Quality control is where a business implements systems designed to check for quality, usually at the end of a production process.

Key terms

Quality is delivering a high standard product or service to the consumer.

Quality assurance is where the business builds quality control into every single stage and aspect of production rather than checking for quality at the end and making quality the job of a few individuals or a department.

Quality control is where a business implements systems designed to check for quality, usually at the end of a production process.

Total quality management (TQM) is a system of promoting and checking quality at every stage of the production process, with all employees taking responsibility for assuring quality.

Traditional quality control involves checking for quality at the end of the production process by quality controllers.

Chapter 2.3.4

The sales process

Aims

By the end of this chapter, students should be able to understand:

- the sales process.
- the importance to businesses of providing good customer service.

The sales process

The sales process consists of all the steps involved in selling a product or providing a service to a customer. The sales process includes the following:

- Initial engagement with the customer.
- Communicating product knowledge.
- Speed and efficiency of customer service.
- Response to customer feedback.
- Post-sales service.

Product knowledge

It is essential for a sales person to have good knowledge of the product or service they are selling so that they can answer customer questions and promote the product or service in question. This is important as a customer will tell friends and family about positive and negative customer service experiences. It is essential, therefore, that the sales process is efficient and staff are well-trained (see Chapter 2.5.3). Comments about customer service travel quickly through word-of-mouth and can impact a business's reputation both positively and negatively.

Speed and efficiency of service

Speed and efficiency of service is important. For example, Deliveroo "promises to bring the world's local restaurants into everyone's home or office – fast." (https://deliveroo.co.uk/faq)

To remain competitive a business such as Deliveroo must fulfill its promise to 'deliver food fast' to retain customers and keep ahead of competition. If it does not do so customers may be dissatisfied. However, a quick and effective response from Deliveroo to a dissatisfied customer helps to retain customers and enhance their reputation as a good business. For example, a late delivery from Deliveroo could result in an apology from Deliveroo and a discount code for a customer's next purchase.

When buying goods online customers are informed about how long it takes for delivery, details of the return and exchange policies and there are often links to customer reviews about the products and services supplied. A website may have an online chat function allowing customers to type their questions and receive an immediate answer. This is common on hotel and car websites and allows questions to be answered quickly.

Customer engagement

Customer engagement is the process of:

- building relationships with customers by communicating with them.
- adapting the level of service to keep customers satisfied.
- making customers loyal and hopefully good ambassadors for the product or brand.

Many businesses now use social media as a means of communicating with customers but, of course, communication often takes place face-to-face.

Examples of customer engagement

- Greeting regular customers by name and making personal recommendations.
- Providing good customer service in the shop.
- Amazon tracks what customers buy and gives them recommendations based on other people who purchased the same product.
- Google creates personalised adverts based on an individual's browsing history.
- Many businesses offer store cards and the application process requires customers to give their personal details to the shop which can subsequently track orders and collect data about customers.
- Collection of customer email addresses also allows businesses to send personalised emails containing information about promotions, new products and special offers and allows the shop to ask for feedback.

Responses to customer feedback

Responding quickly and effectively to customer feedback is another way to engage customers and keep them happy. Often customers who have had their issues dealt with efficiently and effectively will remain loyal to a business. The opposite will happen if there are long delays or even no response to complaints.

For example, a restaurant which takes an excessive amount of time to serve meals to customers but responds by not charging for the meal will likely keep customers happy and they will return. In contrast if no compensation is given for a long wait the customers will leave the restaurant dissatisfied and may write a poor review online and tell their friends not to go to the restaurant. This may deter people from visiting the restaurant in the future.

Customer feedback may be gathered using a questionnaire or survey to be completed in person or online. Businesses may choose to follow up complaints with customers or may thank them for positive reviews in response to customer feedback. For example, online hotel booking sites often contain reviews about hotels written by customers. Positive reviews are sometimes followed by a personal thank you from the hotel manager. Equally, online complaints may be followed up with a public response to the author from the hotel manager which is visible to the public online. Most online stores automatically ask for a rating after a purchase has been received.

Customers' feedback may be gathered in person, for example, the manager of a restaurant may visit tables asking customers if their experience has been positive. This allows them to fix any immediate problems and provides a personalised service to customers.

App based businesses such as Uber and Airbnb ask customers for a rating after providing a car journey or accommodation. Uber and Airbnb customers may also be rated by the Uber driver and Airbnb host but they will not be able to see the review about them until they have posted a review of their experience. This acts as an incentive for customers to complete the review process. The reviews and ratings are available for future buyers and sellers of Airbnb and Uber services.

Communication with businesses is extremely important and some businesses provide 24 hour telephone customer service. Credit card companies and banks often provide this facility using call centres located overseas. Other businesses which use this facility include computer manufacturers, mobile phone service providers and the NHS 111 24-hour helpline is a government funded helpline to assist people 24 hours a day with non-emergency questions about health issues. Some businesses, such as hotels and car hire firms, have a 'live chat' function on their website which allows customers or perspective customers to type their questions and receive an immediate response.

It is vital for businesses to respond quickly to complaints. Information is shared very quickly through social media and complaints that are dealt with swiftly and effectively will hopefully allow the business to be viewed favourably.

Large businesses such as Toyota have a section on their website where customers can ask questions and lodge complaints.

Post-sales service

Service does not finish after purchase. **Post-sales service** occurs when customers have taken ownership of a good or receiving a service. Legally goods must be as described and fit for purpose so a faulty product can be returned to the shop or manufacturer for replacement or repair. Electrical products usually have a 12-month warranty and if the product stops working within this time period it will be repaired or replaced free of charge. For example, Apple shops offer repairs and replacements and free tutorials for Apple customers. Phillips has a website containing product information and answers to frequently asked questions about products. Phillips also has a good repair service and communicates with customers over the phone, online and in their service centres. Internet and electricity providers need to ensure that their customers receive a good service and should offer customer support over the phone and a repair service.

Large businesses such as Toyota have a section on their website where customers can ask questions and lodge complaints. https://www.toyota.com/support/contact-us. This allows customers to contact Toyota 24/7.

The importance to businesses of providing good customer service

Getting customers to buy goods and services is an extremely important part of any business. The sales process can take place face-to-face, over the phone or online.

Good customer service:

- improves a business' reputation.
- may set them apart from competitors.
- retains loyal customers.
- attracts new customers.

Customers are the source of sales revenue for a business and therefore without customers there will be no business. It is extremely important to provide good service to attract and retain customers who will in turn tell others about the good customer service verbally (word-of-mouth) or using online platforms.

Exam style question 1

1. Explain one advantage to a business of providing good customer service. *(3 marks)*
2. Explain one disadvantage to a business of providing poor customer service. *(3 marks)*

Exam style question 2

Francis Jones runs a dog day care business which acts as a nursery for dog owners who work and do not wish to leave the dog alone at home all day. Francis gets most of his business through personal recommendations from existing customers but recently has received a few complaints and some customers have decided to no longer use his services.

1. Define the term customer engagement. *(2 marks)*
2. Explain the reasons why providing good customer service is important to Francis. *(3 marks)*
3. Francis is trying to decide whether to ask customers to complete a feedback survey online or to talk to customers in person about the quality of dog day care. Justify which option would be best for Francis. *(9 marks)*

Chapter review questions

1. Explain why it is important for sellers of a product to have good product knowledge.
2. Explain what is meant by customer engagement.
3. Identify two ways businesses gain feedback from their customers.
4. Describe why it is important for businesses to respond quickly to customer feedback.
5. Give an example of post-sales service.
6. Explain the importance of good customer service for a business.

Key terms

Customer engagement is the process of building relationships with customers by communicating with them and adapting the level of service to keep them satisfied, make them loyal and hopefully become ambassadors of the product or brand.

Post-sales service is customer care and engagement given after customers have taken ownership of a good or after-service.

Chapter 2.4.1

Business calculations

Aims

By the end of this chapter, students should be able to understand:

- the concept and calculation of gross profit and net profit.
- the calculation and interpretation of gross profit margin, net profit margin and average rate of return.

Gross profit and net profit

The **trading account** is a financial document that shows the difference between a firm's sales revenues and its direct costs, i.e. it shows the value of a firm's **gross profit**. Profit is made when sales revenues exceed the costs of goods sold. If costs are greater than revenues, then the business makes a **loss**. Businesses must make a profit to survive in the long run.

Gross profit = Sales revenue – Cost of goods sold

Sales revenue is the value of the goods sold by a business (see Chapter 1.3.2). It is calculated by multiplying the selling price by the number of units sold. As the name suggests, the **cost of goods sold** refer to a firm's direct costs of producing or selling goods.

Suppose that Ashworth Shoes Ltd. bought its stock from a supplier at an average cost of £40 per pair and sold the shoes to customers at an average price of £60. The trading account then shows the firm makes a gross profit of £20 per sale. If the firm sells 200 pairs of shoes in a given time period, the trading account would be shown as:

Trading account for Ashworth Shoes Ltd.:

Sales revenue	=	£12,000	(200 x £60)
Less Cost of goods sold	=	£8,000	(200 x £40)
Gross profit	=	**£4,000**	

The **profit and loss account** (or P&L account) is a financial document used to show the value of net profit (or loss) made by a business during a specified time period. It is usually produced once a year. The P&L account continues from the trading account and shows the value of a firm's **net profit**.

Net profit = Gross profit – Expenses

Expenses are indirect costs of a business (see Chapter 1.3.2). They vary between businesses but will typically include spending on: rent, salaries, utility bills (gas, electricity and water), advertising costs, insurance premiums and interest on bank loans. Suppose the expenses of Ashworth Shoes Ltd. amounts to £1,800 in the given time period. The firm's profit and loss account would then be presented as shown below:

Profit and loss account for Ashworth Shoes Ltd.:

Sales revenue	=	£12,000
Less Cost of goods sold	=	£8,000
Gross profit	=	£4,000
Less Expenses	=	£1,800
Net Profit	=	**£2,200**

The final part of the P&L account is to distribute the net profit. For limited companies (see Chapter 1.4.1), net profit can be distributed in three ways:

- **Taxation** paid to the government.
- **Dividends** paid to shareholders.
- **Retained profit** as a source of internal finance (see Chapter 1.3.4) for business use.

Gross profit is the difference between the value of a firm's sales revenue and its cost of purchasing those products for sale.

Net profit is the value of a firm's profit after both cost of goods sold and expenses have been deducted.

Gross profit margin and net profit margin

Ratio analysis is a quantitative technique that uses the financial performance of a business to judge success (or failures). A ratio is simply one number expressed in terms of another. When looking at numbers in isolation, managers might not get the full picture. For example, it is difficult to judge the financial performance of two rival firms that earn the same amount of profit:

Company A: net profit = £100,000

Company B: net profit = £100,000

However, if we compare these figures to the respective company's sales figures, a different picture is found:

Company A: sales revenue = £500,000

Company B: sales revenue = £1,000,000

$$\textbf{Net profit margin} = \frac{\textbf{Net profit}}{\textbf{Sales revenue}} \times \textbf{100\%}$$

$$\textbf{Net profit margin Company A} = \frac{£100,000}{£500,000} \times 100\% = 20\%$$

$$\textbf{Net profit margin Company B} = \frac{£100,000}{£1,000,000} \times 100\% = 10\%$$

In this case, it is clear that Company A has performed better since it has generated the same value of profit from half the sales revenue of its competitor. By contrast, it seems that Company B has more difficulty in managing its costs.

Ratio analysis can help to inform internal and external stakeholders (see Chapter 1.5.1) about the following:

- how well a business is doing, such as by comparing the profitability of the organisation over time.
- provide insight into whether the business could perform better, perhaps by comparing its financial performance with that of rivals (a process known as **benchmarking**).
- for owners (shareholders) and investors, ratio analysis can provide information on whether their investment was worthwhile.

The **gross profit margin** (**GPM**) calculates the percentage of sales revenue that is gross profit. For example, a gross profit ratio of 65% means that for every £100 of sales revenue, the firm earns £65 gross profit. The other 35% is attributed to the cost of goods sold (see Chapter 1.3.2). Hence, the higher the ratio, the better it is for the business.

$$\textbf{Gross profit margin} = \frac{\textbf{Gross profit}}{\textbf{Sales revenue}} \times \textbf{100\%}$$

For example, if Kingman Book Store has sales revenue of £150,000 and its cost of goods sold is £70,000 then its gross profit would be £150,000 – £70,000 = £80,000. Hence, its gross profit ratio is £80,000 / £150,000 = 53.33%.

A higher gross profit ratio can be achieved by earning a greater gross profit and/or reduced costs of production. Examples include:

- A higher price generates a greater profit margin (the difference between selling price and the direct costs).
- A fall in the cost of goods sold also raises the profit margin.
- Improved cost control.
- Using product extension strategies or launching new products (see Chapter 4.2) to boost revenue and hence profits.

Exam style question 1

Profit and loss account for Kingman Book Store:

	Sept (£)	**Oct (£)**	**Nov (£)**	**Dec (£)**
Sales revenue	15,000		10,500	16,000
Cost of goods sold	7,200	5,980		7,520
Gross profit		5,520	4,725	8,480
Gross profit margin		48%		

(a) Define the term 'gross profit margin'. *(2 marks)*

(b) Calculate the missing figures in the above table and show all workings. *(10 marks)*

(c) Analyse the performance of Kingman Book Store during the given time period. *(6 marks)*

The **net profit margin** calculates the percentage of sales revenue that is net profit. For example, a net profit ratio of 35% means that for every £100 of sales revenue, the firm earns £35 net profit. The other 65% is comprised of both the cost of goods sold and the firm's expenses (see Chapter 1.3.2). The difference between a firm's gross and net profit margins indicates its ability to control expenses (overheads). Hence, the higher the ratio, the better it is for the business.

$$\textbf{Net profit margin} = \frac{\textbf{Net profit}}{\textbf{Sales revenue}} \times 100\%$$

For example, consider the following figures for Kingman Book Store:

Sales revenue	£150,000
less Cost of goods sold	£70,000
Gross profit	£80,000
less Expenses	£35,000
Net profit	£45,000

The net profit ratio would be

$$\frac{£45,000}{£150,000} = 30\%$$

A higher net profit ratio can be achieved by better control of overheads such as rent and insurance costs. The higher the ratio, the more efficient the business is in managing its expenses.

Exam style question 2

Study the data in the table below for two firms in direct competition and answer the questions that follow:

Business	**Gross profit margin**	**Net profit margin**
Zawada Ltd.	40%	20%
Chan Corp.	45%	23%

(a) Define the term 'net profit margin'. *(2 marks)*

(b) Using the financial information provided, justify whether Zawada Ltd. or Chan Corp. has performed better. *(6 marks)*

Exam style question 3

Karoo Florists Ltd. supplies fresh flowers to restaurants, hotels and other businesses in Melbourne, Australia. The company's accountant has provided the following financial information:

Sales revenue = £18,960

Cost of goods sold = £6,320

Expenses = £6,000

(a) Define the term 'expenses'. *(2 marks)*

(b) From the above information, calculate the (i) gross and (ii) net profit of the company. *(4 marks)*

(c) In the previous year, the company's gross profit was £11,450 and its net profit was £6,040. Calculate the gross profit margin and net profit margins for both years. *(4 marks)*

(d) Analyse the performance of Karoo Florists Ltd. Over the past two years. *(6 marks)*

Average rate of return (ARR)

The rate of return on an investment is the percentage of profit (return) earned on the amount of funds invested in the business. To calculate the average rate of return of a business:

$$\textbf{Average rate of return (\%)} = \frac{\textbf{Average annual profit (total profit/number of years)}}{\textbf{Cost of investment}} \times 100\%$$

Worked example

Two entrepreneurs invested £150,000 in a hairdressers located in Cambridge. The profits earned were as follows:

Year	Profit (£'000)
1	35
2	38
3	45
4	40
5	39

Calculate the Average Rate of Return (ARR) on the investment.

$$\text{ARR (\%)} = \frac{\text{Average annual profit}}{\text{Cost of investment}} \times 100\%$$

$$= \frac{(35 + 38 + 45 + 40 + 39)/5}{150} \times 100\%$$

$$= \frac{39.5}{150} \times 100\%$$

$$= \mathbf{26.3\%}$$

The £150,000 investment in the hairdressers has created a return of 26.3% per year. This looks like a healthy return at face value but in order to decide whether this is true it is necessary to compare the return on the investment to what could have been earned elsewhere. For example, if the £150,000 was saved in a bank how much interest could it have earned? Clearly in times of low interest rates the investment in the hairdressers is much greater than what could have been earned in a bank account. It is however important to compare the ARR of the hairdressers with that of a similar business in the same industry to determine whether investment in the hairdresser was worthwhile. 26.3% is a high ARR.

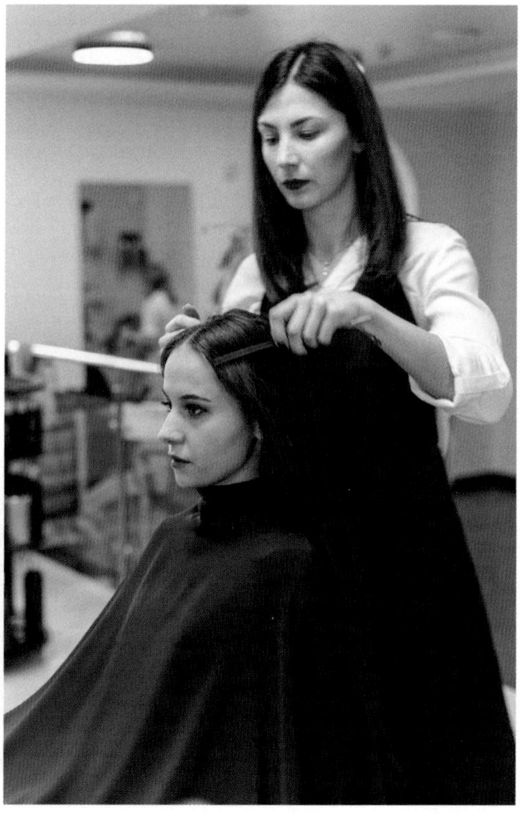

Exam style question 4

The Riverside Golf Driving Range cost £2,000,000 to construct. It is open for individual use and golf lessons. It is open seven days per week and been popular since it opened 6 years ago. The profit figures are as follows:

Year	Profit (£'000)
1	1500
2	1900
3	2000
4	2100
5	2000
6	2150

(a) Calculate the Average Rate of Return (%) of Riverside Golf Driving Range. *(4 marks)*

(b) Identify two other types of information which would help the business to decide whether the investment has been worthwhile. *(2 marks)*

Chapter review questions

1. State the formula for gross and net profit margins.
2. Distinguish between the gross and net profit margins.
3. Explain why a business would wish to calculate gross profit margin.
4. Explain what the net profit margin reveals about a business.
5. What is the formula for calculating the average rate of return (ARR)?
6. What does the ARR tell you about a business performance.

Key terms

Average rate of return (%) $= \dfrac{\text{Average annual profit (total profit/number of years)}}{\text{Cost of investment}} \times 100\%$

Gross profit is the difference between the value of a firm's sales revenue and its cost of purchasing those products for sale.

Gross profit margin (**GPM**) calculates a firm's gross profit as a percentage of its sales revenue. For example, a gross profit ratio of 75% means that for every £100 of sales revenue, the firm earns £75 gross profit.

Gross profit margin $= \dfrac{\text{Gross profit}}{\text{Sales revenue}} \times 100\%$

Net profit is the value of a firm's profit after both cost of goods sold and expenses have been deducted.

Net profit margin (**NPM**) calculates the percentage of sales revenue that is net profit, after all costs have been paid for. So, a net profit ratio of 45% means that for every £100 of sales revenue, the firm earns £45 net profit.

Net profit margin $= \dfrac{\text{Net profit}}{\text{Sales revenue}} \times 100\%$

Trading, Profit and Loss account is a financial statement used to show the value of gross profit and net profit (or loss) made by a business during a specified time period.

Chapter 2.4.2

Understanding business performance

Aims

By the end of this chapter, students should be able to understand:

- the use and interpretation of quantitative business data to support, inform and justify business decisions.
- the use and limitations of financial information.

The use and interpretation of quantitative business data: Information from graphs and charts

Quantitative business data is numerical data used to support, inform and justify business decisions. Examples include: gross and net profit figures, sales revenue, costs, market share and the number of firms in a market.

Figure 2.4.2a: Net profit Whitstables Ltd. (£'000)

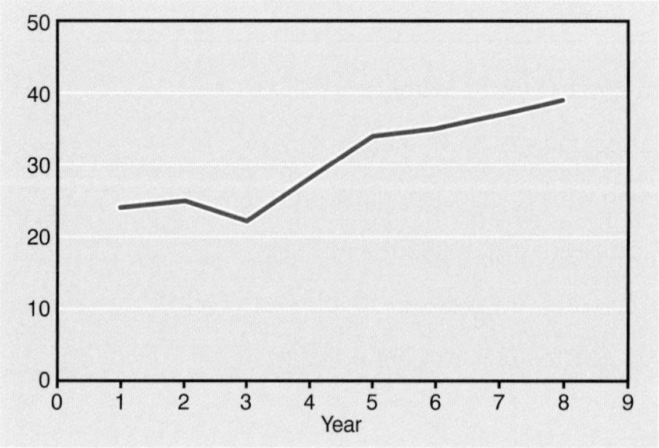

Figure 2.4.2a shows net profit earned by a shop called Whitstables Ltd., which sells children's furniture, over the past eight years of operation. Net profits have increased over the time period with a slight decrease between years 2 and 3. Total net profit earned during the eight years of operation is £244,000. Growth in profits has slowed down in the past three years but they are still rising steadily and hopefully the trend will continue into the future.

Increasing profits may be indicative of the following:

- Increasing market share.
- Decrease in the number of competitors.
- Increasing popularity of the type of children's furniture sold and therefore increase in sales.
- Decrease in costs of business.

A **decision** may be taken to expand the business based on increasing profits or the owner of the business may be content with steadily rising profits.

Figure 2.4.2b: Product life cycle of selfie sticks, sales revenue (£'000)

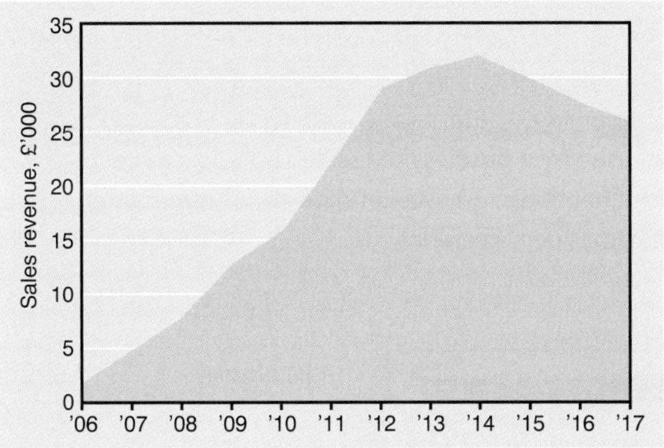

The product life cycle of selfie sticks

The product life cycle (see Chapter 2.2.1) of a business can be used to inform and support decisions about pricing and promotional strategies and whether the business should use extension strategies to lengthen the life of the product. A business may also try to identify reasons for decreases in sales. In the case of the selfie stick it may be a trend which is over. Legislation to ban use of selfie sticks in public places such as theme parks may have decreased demand for them.

Financial data

Table 2.4.2a

Financial Data	Business A	Business B	Business C
Net profit margin	22%	25%	31%
Gross profit margin	35%	36%	40%
Average rate of return	14%	17%	11%

Businesses A, B and C are all similar sized hairdressers based in Manchester city centre.

Analysis of the gross and net profit margins (see Chapter 2.4.1) suggest that Business C is the most profitable as it has the highest ratio of net and gross profit to sales revenue of all three businesses.

Business B has a higher average rate of return (see Chapter 2.4.1) than business A and C. This suggests that the average annual profit compared to the total amount of funds invested in the business is highest for Business B. In other words, the funds invested in Business B are more efficient at producing profits than the other two businesses. A potential investor would study the financial data to decide which business, if any, to invest in. An investor would also use qualitative data to inform and support their decision.

Marketing data

Marketing data consists of many types of information about the industry and related industries a business operates in. Examples include:

- Customer rankings of business in an industry.
- Results of market research.
- Spending by businesses on digital media.

Marketing data helps businesses to compare themselves to other businesses. Large businesses may buy data about the industry in which they operate from professional market research companies such as Mintel. The data may contain important information about their competitors which can inform, justify or support decisions about the future of the business or how they should adapt their marketing mix.

Market data

Market data is data on the market in which a business operates, for example, market share, total value of the market and number of firms in the market. Figure 2.4.2c shows the number of firms in a market. Firm A is the market leader and the three largest firms in the industry have approximately 52% of the market. This type of information may be used by a business to create strategies to keep abreast with competitors by altering its marketing mix (see Chapter 2.2.5). Market data also includes information about growth and potential sales inform and support business decisions.

Figure 2.4.2c

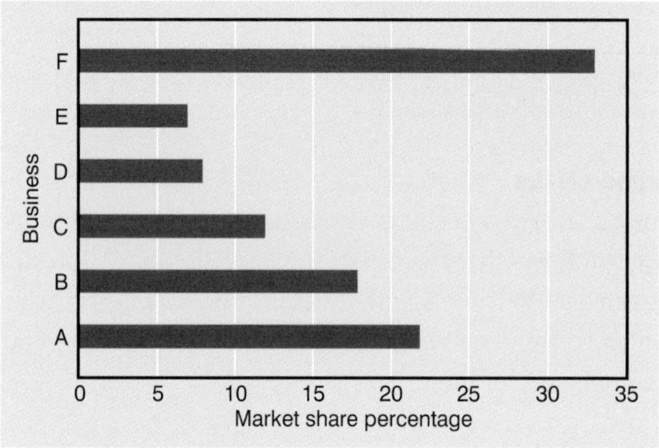

Business	Market Share %
A	22
B	18
C	12
D	8
E	7
F Others	33

Exam style question 1

Sales revenue of Nandita's chiropody practice, £'000

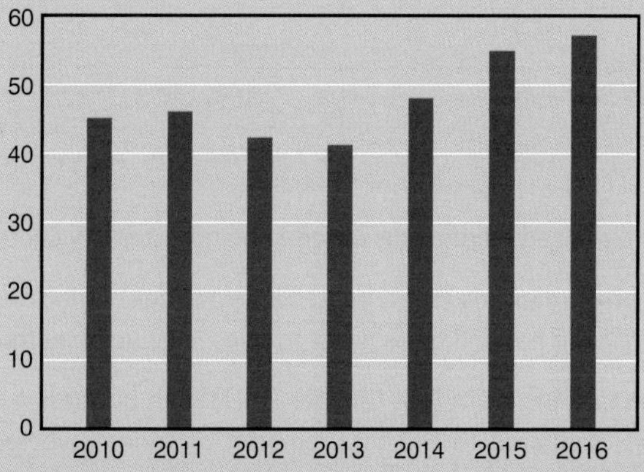

Nandita is a chiropodist who runs her own practice based in Glasgow. There are a number of chiropodists in the city but Nandita has built up a good client base and enjoys working from a clinic in which are based a number of other health practitioners including a chiropractor and physiotherapist. Each practitioner shares the costs of the renting the premises, cleaning, wages of the receptionist and other running costs. Nandita has studied the figures and has determined that in 2013 her father died and she took an extended period of compassionate leave. This explains the decrease in sales revenue in 2013.

1. Outline the trend in Nandita's sales revenue since 2010. *(3 marks)*

2 Analyse Nandita's decision in 2014 to increase the amount she charges patients per consultation. *(6 marks)*

Understanding business performance and making business decisions

Analysis of a combination of financial, marketing and market data allows firms to make decisions about the following:

- Whether to adapt marketing mix in response to changing market conditions (see Chapter 2.2.5).
- Whether to adapt marketing mix in response to actions of competitors (see Chapter 2.2.5).
- Whether to expand business or downsize.
- Whether to open new branches or relocate.

Use and limitations of financial analysis

Although analysis of financial data can provide very useful information for management decision-making, there are several limitations, which include:

- Analysis is conducted using past financial results which might not indicate how the business will perform in future.
- Historical comparisons of financial information do not necessarily account for changes in the costs of production over time, which can be affected by inflation (see Chapter 1.5.4). Similarly, exchange rates can also affect the level of sales revenue and profits for businesses engaged in international trade (see Chapter 1.5.4).
- It is also important to compare like-with-like. Most managers will want to compare gross and net profit margins of businesses in the same industry. Different accounting practices are used in different parts of the world, so caution must be used when comparing ratios of businesses in different countries.
- Qualitative factors that affect decision-making (such as management preferences or the impact of decisions on staff morale) are ignored in ratio analysis.

Limitations of marketing and market data

Although marketing and market data informs many business decisions it has limitations which include:

- Markets are constantly changing and data may be out-of-date.
- Data sources may be unreliable.
- Projections of future sales may be prove to be inaccurate.

Chapter review questions

1. Explain the difference between quantitative and qualitative data.
2. Give three examples of financial data which may be used to judge the performance of a business.
3. Outline reasons why market data can help to inform business decisions.
4. Give an example of marketing data which may be used to inform business decisions to adapt the marketing mix.
5. Give an example of market data which could support a business decision.
6. Explain the limitations of using financial data to understand business performance.
7. Explain the limitations of using financial data in making business decisions.

Key terms

Financial data – is quantitative data about the business which may include: gross and net profit, sales revenue and breakeven point.

Market data – is data on the market in which a business operates, for example, market share, total value of the market and number of firms in the market.

Marketing data – consists of many types of information about the industry a business operates in, the business itself and related industries e.g. customer rankings of businesses in an industry and the results of market research.

Qualitative data is data which does not consist of numbers and may consist of results of interviews, observation.

Quantitative business data is numerical data which may consist of financial data, market share and number of firms in an industry.

Chapter 2.5.1

Organisational structures

Aims

By the end of this chapter, students should be able to understand:

- different organisational structures and when each are appropriate.
- the importance of effective communication.
- different ways of working.

Organisational structure

Fresh Recruitment Ltd. is a recruitment agency which recruits suitable workers for businesses and finds appropriate jobs for people seeking work. It has the following organisational structure:

Figure 2.5.1a

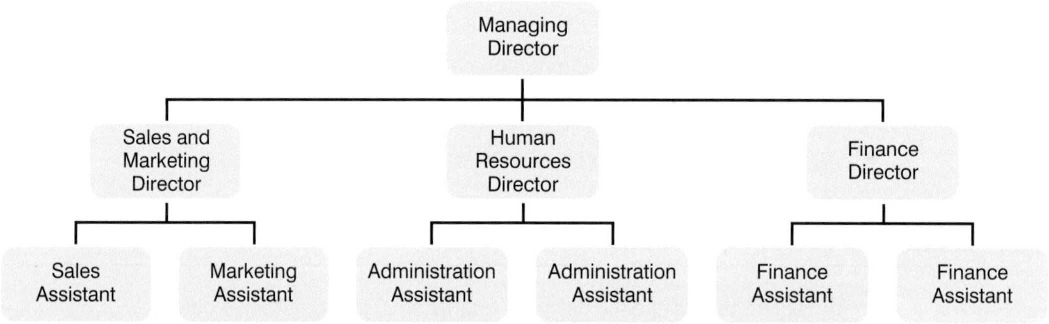

There are 3 levels in the **hierarchy** (number of layers in the organisational structure).

The army is a good example of an organisation with a **highly hierarchical organisational structure**, which has many layers between employees at the top and bottom of the organisation.

A **flat organisational structure** would have fewer levels of hierarchy. Tech companies usually operate with such a structure.

Advantages of a flat structure	Disadvantages of a flat structure
Vertical communication can be quick and efficient as messages need not be passed down a long chain of command.	A short chain of command implies large numbers of managers and may impact adversely upon the nature and frequency of communication between workers and line managers.
Communication between workers may lead to greater motivation and team work.	

Advantages of a hierarchical structure	Disadvantages of a hierarchical structure
Employees may aspire to promotion as there is clear progression through the company.	Decisions may take a long time as there are many levels in the hierarchy.
Staff might work better in smaller teams (a feature of organisations with a long chain of command) rather than in large disparate teams (common in organisations with a short chain of command).	Communication may be time consuming as there are many layers in the hierarchy. Information may be distorted due to the length of the communication chain.

McDonald's use a highly centralised organisational structure that leaves little freedom for restaurant managers to take decisions.

Centralised and decentralised structures

In **centralised organisations** the majority of decisions are made by the most senior managers and then passed down through the hierarchy. Managing a business in this way gives great control to the key decision makers but can lead to poor decisions made remotely by people who have little understanding of the situation 'on the ground'.

McDonald's use a highly centralised organisational structure that leaves little freedom for restaurant managers to take decisions. This might be demotivating for some managers and may even cost revenue and profit in some cases where a manager has great vision and business acumen. However, McDonald's prizes consistency in the brand over allowing managers such freedoms. It is hard to argue that their approach is not a successful one!

Decentralised organisations delegate decision making to the appropriate areas of the business. This can mean less control for the senior management but it allows for decisions to be made at the right time by the right individual with the correct grasp of the problem.

Supermarkets can be examples of decentralised organisations. Most supermarkets have a store manager who is granted the autonomy to make decisions about things such as product ranges and promotional strategies. As well as the motivational impact of being trusted to manage it makes sense for a store manager in St Ives to make such decisions as the trading conditions in Cornwall might be very different from those that are prevalent in London where the head office is located.

Exam style question 1

Examine the benefits to a smartphone app developer of having a decentralised organisational structure. *(6 marks)*

The importance of effective communication

Communication – The receiver may give feedback to the sender (two-way communication) or may not (one-way communication).

Good communication is important because:

1. It creates good relationships between:
   (a) individuals and other business organisations, e.g. customers and suppliers
   (b) employees and management who are internal to the business.
2. Clear instructions from a manager to a subordinate will mean that a task is carried out correctly.
3. Accurate, honest advertising from a business will attract and hopefully satisfy customers.
4. A correct response to a customer complaint will solve the problem and satisfy the customer.

Insufficient communication can impact on **efficiency and motivation** for a variety of reasons:

- Communicating insufficient information about the merits of your product can lead to higher numbers of complaints which cost time and resources to resolve.
- If insufficient or inaccurate messages are passed through the business, then this can prevent workers from getting it 'right first time' and resources might be wasted correcting mistakes.
- Insufficient messages can leave workers unclear as to what is expected of them. This can demotivate staff and demotivated workers are likely to be less productive.
- Workers who feel that they are being deliberately 'kept out of the loop' are likely to feel as though their opinion is not counted and may fear that secretive management is a threat to their security. This, again, is likely to reduce levels of motivation and damage productivity.

Excessive communication can impact on efficiency and motivation for a variety of reasons:

- Workers that are bombarded with emails may find it difficult to focus their attention on the task that they are being paid to do and this may reduce productivity and efficiency.
- Workers that have to deal with excessive communications may find it difficult to distinguish between messages that are urgent and those that are trivial. Key tasks might be deprioritised and a business might be less efficient as a result. To combat this, many businesses have started to designate days of the week as 'no email' days to try to allow workers to clear inboxes and focus more on the task in hand.
- Employees that are messaged too often by their managers may feel as though they are being tightly monitored and not trusted to get on with the job. This can lead to a loss of motivation.

Barriers to effective communication

Poor communication with external customers and suppliers can damage the reputation of a company. The business may lose customers and be unable to compete with its competitors.

Reasons for poor communication (barriers to communication) include:

1. **Technical language** (jargon) used in the message may not be understood by the receiver.
2. The wrong **medium** was chosen e.g. a meeting to inform staff about possible loss of jobs would be preferable to sending this information in a text message.
3. The **message** may be too long or unclearly conveyed.
4. There may be no opportunity for **feedback** as a decision has already been taken.
5. The **receiver** may not read the message or receive the message, for example. an email might be sent directly to a spam folder or a text message deleted by accident.

Different ways of working: part-time, full-time and flexible hours

Part time employment is where a worker works fewer hours per week than a full time contract. Typically, a part time contract is less than 30 hours of employment. Part time workers often do not have the same rights as full time staff and can be employed on rotational shifts to, for example, support full time staff during busy periods.

Full time employment is when an employee works a minimum number of hours as defined by the employer. A standard working week in the UK would be considered, on average, to be based on a 9am to 5pm working day from Monday to Friday. Of course, many jobs work shift patterns and therefore the hours of work are different but the number of hours considered to be full time would be in the region of 35-40 hours for most jobs in the UK. Full time work also implies that workers have a single job and a single employer and it is usually the case that an employer provides the full time employee with additional benefits such as certain pension rights or the provision of sick pay. Of course, hiring a full time worker might cost more due to these benefits, but a securely employed worker is likely to be more motivated to work and committed to the organisation.

Flexible hours may be irregular and varied in order to find a balance between the needs of the business and the availability of the employee.

Flexible hours are where the hours worked differ from the normal business opening hours. This can be an attractive working pattern for those workers who are juggling family commitments with the demands of work. Working hours may be irregular and varied in order to find a balance between the needs of the business and the availability of the employee. Workers in the UK have a right to request flexible working, subject to certain qualifying criteria such as length of service and employers need to demonstrate sound business reasons for denying a request.

Permanent contracts of employment are contracts that run indefinitely until such a time as the employee and/or the employer no longer wishes it to run and has provided adequate notice to end the contract. Having said that, an employer cannot end the contract unless it is broken in accordance with the relevant laws governing the employment of workers in the UK.

Temporary contracts are for workers who are employed for a fixed period of time. At the end of the period both parties are freed from the terms of the contract. That said, in many cases a worker that has performed well in a temporary post will be made permanent.

Freelance contracts are given by firms to individuals that work for them on a self-employed basis as contractors. The use of this type of labour has been controversial in the UK as companies such as Uber have claimed that their drivers are freelance employees to whom they simply provide technology to help them find taxi fares. They do this because it means they do not have to give them any benefits such as sick pay or holiday pay and no minimum guaranteed hours apply. This is good for Uber's efficiency but it has harmed their reputation in the eyes of some consumers.

The impact of technology on ways of working

Technology can enhance productivity and **efficiency** by allowing workers to work in new ways. For example, workers can work on the daily commute and arrive to work having already checked emails and responded to customer queries. Workers can download key documents from the cloud that enable them to get to work on tasks without having to wait for hard copies of files.

Remote working refers to the growing trend for people to carry out their job away from the office. It has allowed workers in many industries to be able to complete tasks and conduct business from home. This has enabled more flexible working patterns and has allowed employees to maintain a better work life balance through managing domestic commitments around work. It has also allowed for the outsourcing of services such as proofreading to workers anywhere in the world.

Exam style question

Yodel is a delivery courier service that delivers packages for retailers such as Amazon. Justify whether Yodel should employ their delivery drivers on a full time or freelance basis. *(9 marks)*

Chapter review questions

1. Define the term 'hierarchy'
2. Give two advantages of a flat organisational structure.
3. Explain why insufficient communication can lead to a rise in the costs of business.
4. Why can excessive communication reduce the motivation of employees?
5. Explain three barriers to effective communication.
6. Explain the difference between full time and part time working hours.
7. Explain the term 'freelance contract'.
8. Explain two ways in which technology has led to new ways of working.
9. How can remote working increase business efficiency?

Key terms

Centralised organisational structures are where the majority of decisions are made by the most senior managers and then passed down through the hierarchy.

Communication receiver may give feedback to the sender (two-way communication or may not (one-way communication).

Decentralised organisational structures delegate decision making to the appropriate areas of the business.

Flat organisational structures have only a few layers in the hierarchy, for example, three layers.

Flexible hours are where the hours worked differ from the normal business opening hours.

Freelance contracts are given by firms to individuals that work for them on a self-employed basis such as contractors or consultants.

Full time employment is when an employee works a minimum number of hours as defined by the employer.

Hierarchical organisational structures have many layers to the hierarchy and there is a distance between the CEO and employees at the bottom of the hierarchy.

Hierarchy is the number of levels in the organisational structure.

Part time employment is where a worker works fewer hours per week than a full time contract.

Permanent contracts of employment run indefinitely until such a time as the employee and/or the employer no longer wishes it to run.

Remote working refers to the growing trend for people to use technology to carry out their job away from the office.

Temporary contracts are for workers who are employed temporarily, for a fixed period of time only.

Chapter 2.5.2

Effective recruitment

Aims

By the end of this chapter, students should be able to understand:

- different job roles and responsibilities.
- how businesses recruit people.

Different job roles and responsibilities

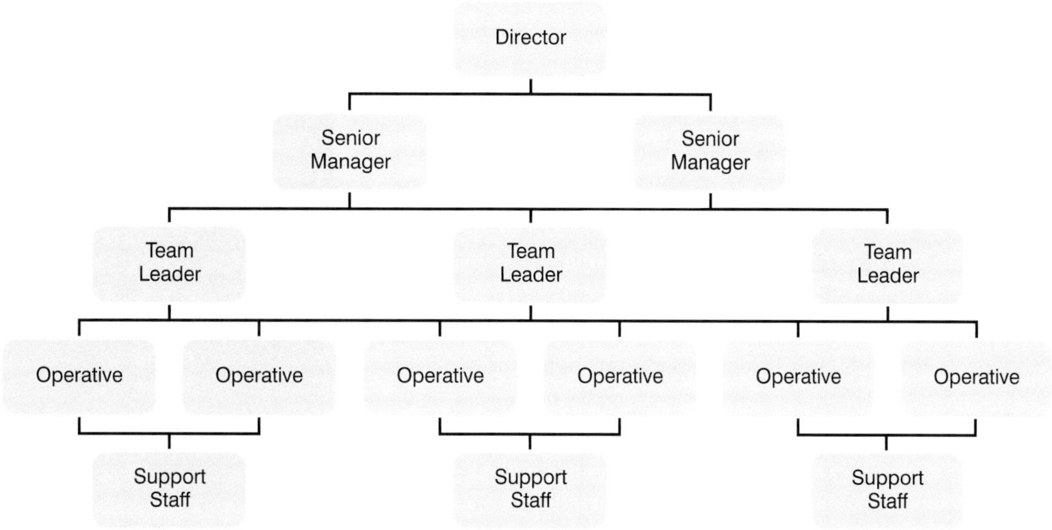

Directors are the main decision makers and leaders of the business. They are appointed to run strategic parts of the business and shareholders (owners of the business) vote at the AGM (annual general meeting) on whether to retain or replace the directors. Directors are at the top of the hierarchy (see Chapter 2.5.1) in the business.

Senior managers are appointed to lead teams or departments within a business. For example, a large firm of accountants may have a number of senior leaders who each lead a different team of accountants and trainee accountants. Alternatively, a senior manager may be in charge of a department such as the finance, marketing or human resource department. Large organisations with many branches in different geographical locations will appoint a manager at each location.

Supervisors/team leaders report to the senior managers and lead small teams of people. A team leader working in McDonald's will be responsible for making sure that their team is working efficiently during a shift. They will report to the manager of the restaurant.

Operational staff carry out the actual operations or functions in a business and report to their supervisor/team leader and manager. For example, a waiter in Pizza Express will take orders, serve food and clear tables and report to their team leader/supervisor. A sales assistant in Zara will arrange clothes on shelves, help customers find what they are looking for and work on the changing room. They will report to their supervisors who in turn will report to the manager of the shop.

Support staff are people who support others in an organisation and do not necessarily fit into the traditional hierarchical structure. The ICT department will support all employees by ensuring that their computers are functioning properly and they will look after the ICT system within the organisation. A receptionist will direct telephone calls to individuals, greet visitors and is a communication point for staff. Large organisations will need people to clean and perform maintenance tasks.

How businesses recruit people

A business produces some or all of the following documents when recruiting:

A **job description** is a document that outlines the key duties and responsibilities of the post, where the post fits into the organisational structure (see Chapter 2.5.1), the hours and place of work and any other details and relevant information that a potential applicant might require.

A **person specification** is a description of the ideal candidate in terms of the qualifications, experience and skills that they would need in order to carry out the role effectively. Many businesses will distinguish between those factors that are essential for a successful application and those that are simply desirable. This is a crucial document as it can be a tool that helps the business **shortlist** (select a small number of suitable candidates from the pool of applicants) the right candidates for interview. It also shows potential applicants what the company is looking for and hence limits the number of applications from unsuitable candidates, saving the managers and human resources department time in the process.

Larger businesses often ask job applicants to complete an **application form** so that the information provided about a person's qualifications, work experience, training, letter of application and contact information for referees is in a consistent format and it is easier to compare candidates. It also ensures that they receive all the information they require.

Some businesses will ask candidates to apply by sending in their **CV** (curriculum vitae which means 'course of one's life' in Latin) along with a **letter of application**. The CV is a summary of a candidate's previous work experience, education and training. A CV will also provide contact details of two people who the candidate has worked for previously who will give them a reference and support their application. In the letter of application, a candidate explains reasons why they would like to work for the organisation and why they are suitable for the job they are applying for.

A curriculum vitae is a summary of a candidate's previous work experience, education and training.

Recruitment methods

Most businesses will go through the following steps in order to recruit new employees:

- The Human Resources department will identify that a **vacancy** exists. The reasons this may have arisen are outlined above.
- A **job description** and a **person specification** are prepared.
- The Human Resources department will **advertise** the position in their choice of media. The selection will depend on the factors outlined above.
- After the application deadline has passed, the business will **shortlist** candidates for interview. The number of people on the shortlist will depend on factors such as the resources of the business and the number of posts available.
- Each applicant will have been asked to provide the details of two people who could provide a **reference** to support their application and verify the details of it. The human resources department will contact the referees to gain more information about the shortlisted candidates.
- Shortlisted candidates are next invited to attend an **interview** where they are questioned about their aptitude for the job and are encouraged to ask questions of their own. The purpose is to find a good match between the candidate, the requirements of the role and the corporate culture of the business. Sometimes, candidates will also be asked to complete skills tests or tasks related to the role to further assess their suitability.

- After the interviews the business decides which candidate is best equipped to carry out the role and then makes a **job offer** to him/her. If the candidate accepts there might be some final checks needed such as checking the criminal record of the person offered the job. Once these final checks have been completed, the new employee can be invited to take up the post.

Exam style question 1

Phó Real is a Vietnamese restaurant in Cardiff. The manager has decided that she needs to recruit extra waiting staff to work during busy lunch times and at weekends.

(a) Give two examples of requirements that might be asked for on the person specification. *(2 marks)*

(b) Explain whether the manager should advertise in a national newspaper for new waiting staff. *(4 marks)*

(c) One applicant looks very strong on the basis of her application but has failed to provide the names of two referees. Explain whether this is a problem for Phó Real. *(4 marks)*

Reasons for recruiting employees

There are many reasons why a business might need to recruit workers, including:

- If a firm is **expanding**, for example a retailer might be opening a new store or branch, it is likely it will need to increase its human resources to enable that expansion.
- If workers leave the business or are **dismissed** from their posts then replacements must be found.
- To cover **temporary leave** such as when a company has workers on long-term sick or maternity leave. Short-term replacements may be required.
- If an employee has been promoted then their previous position will be vacated and may need to be filled.

When a business is looking for a new employee they must decide how they plan to recruit that person. They can do this in two ways:

Internal recruitment is where a business fills a vacancy through appointing an existing employee currently occupying a different role in the organisation. There are many advantages to this approach. Firstly, costs to the firm should be reduced in terms of, for example, advertising the position and relocation expenses that may not need to be paid. Secondly, promoting from within and allowing employees to experience different roles within the company are likely to increase morale and motivation as staff members believe that they can achieve their potential within the business. However, often, existing employees simply do not have the necessary set of skills and experience to make this method of recruitment viable and in some cases it might be desirable to bring in an outsider with fresh ideas and ways of doing things.

External recruitment is where a business employs a person from outside the organisation to fill the role. The main advantage of recruitment of this kind is that a business should have a larger pool of applicants to draw from and hence should find a close match in terms of the qualities desired in the new employee.

There are many ways that a business can manage its external recruitment and it might choose a mixture of different methods in order to maximise the chances of recruiting the right candidate. These methods include:

- Government-run **job centres** which match vacancies with suitable people currently unemployed. Job centre staff will often do some of the screening checks on behalf of the company.
- Companies may wish to **advertise** the vacancy in one or many different types of media such as newspapers (local and national), trade journals, magazines, company website, online recruitment websites. When deciding which media to use a company must consider factors such as coverage, response rates, location, and perhaps most importantly of all, cost.

- Private firms called **recruitment agencies** conduct job searches on behalf of job seekers or recruitment campaigns on behalf of companies. Companies use them to screen suitable applicants and carry out the necessary recruitment administration. This service does come at a cost, but it can save a business a lot of time and effort and is a good option for small firms without any expertise in recruitment.
- Where a business needs a very specific set of qualities to fulfil a role effectively it may ask a special type of employment agent known as a **head hunter** to go out and recruit a strong candidate. The candidate will usually already be in a job and so incentive packages are usually offered in order to attract them. These head hunting firms will usually charge the business a commission based on the salary of the new employee they have attracted.
- One attractive method for firms to recruit staff is simply through getting the message out through **word of mouth** that vacancies exist. This is usually done via existing employees. This is especially effective if the job requires less skill and experience as the amount of people that come to hear about the positions may be low.

Exam style question 2

The partner of a large firm of accountants has retired and needs to be replaced.

(a) Discuss whether the firm should recruit internally or externally. *(12 marks)*

Chapter review questions

1. State the responsibilities of the following positions within a business such as H&M or Gap: directors, senior managers, supervisors/team leaders, operational staff and support staff.
2. Outline the reasons for compiling a job description and person specification.
3. What is written in a CV?
4. Why do some businesses ask job applicants to complete an application form?
5. What is the difference between internal and external recruitment methods?
6. Explain the advantages and disadvantages of internal recruitment.
7. Explain the advantages and disadvantages of external recruitment.
8. Explain three reasons why a business might need to recruit a new member of staff.
9. What are the advantages and disadvantages of using a headhunter to recruit a new employee?

Key terms

An **application form** is designed to collect the following information about a person applying for a job: personal details, qualifications, work experience, training, letter of application and contact information for referees.

CV is a summary of a person's previous work experience, education and training.

External recruitment is where the business employs somebody from outside the organisation.

Internal recruitment is where a business employs somebody that is already working within an organisation.

Interviews are question and answer sessions between the business and an applicant designed to find out if an applicant is a strong candidate for a post.

A **job description** is a document that is drawn up in order to show the key roles and responsibilities of a post.

A **person specification** is a document drawn up to describe the attributes that an ideal candidate for a post would possess.

Recruitment is the process of attracting and employing people to carry out roles within the business.

Chapter 2.5.3

Effective training and development

Aims

By the end of this chapter, students should be able to understand:

- how businesses train and develop employees.
- different ways of training and developing employees.
- why businesses train and develop employees.

How businesses train and develop employees

There are many different ways of training and developing employees. **Formal training** is when an employee goes on a training course to learn a particular skill or acquire knowledge. This type of training usually occurs off-the-job. **Apprenticeships** are a type of formal training which occurs when a business employs somebody that does not have all of the skills required for the job and trains them for a period of time until they are skilled in a particular field. Apprenticeships are available in a wide range of industries, from horticulture to public relations. They will usually involve on- and off-the-job training.

Off-the-job training is training undertaken away from the usual place of work. Many large businesses will take the trainee out of the normal working environment and send them to a custom designed training centre for the training. Off-the-job training is often provided by external organisations such as colleges or professional training companies.

Advantages of off-the-job training	Disadvantages of off-the-job training
Will usually lead to a general or industry recognised qualification.	The employee may not value the training and lack the focus and motivation required to learn.
Courses are usually run by experienced, expert trainers. These trainers can train people in the 'softer' skills such as communication and team working that can get neglected when learning on the job.	It might be the case that the manner in which the skills are taught or the material being covered is not really relevant or applicable to the trainee's role.
Some job roles, such as astronauts or soldiers, might be trained exclusively off-the-job but it is more likely that a trainee has an off-the-job component to complement the on-the-job training being done.	The training offered can be a huge cost to the business and the benefits may be realised by a competitor should the employee wish to leave.
Specialist trainers often deliver the course in purpose-built environments where trainees are not sidetracked by emails, phone calls and other distractions endemic in the modern workplace. This allows them to focus on the training and the acquisition of new skills.	
It offers an opportunity for staff to meet and forge links with other departments and sometimes other businesses. This can foster positive work relationships and enhance productivity.	

Informal training is where employees are trained whilst doing the job (on-the-job training) and this type of training does not lead to formal qualifications. There are not many job roles where simply learning by doing, whilst under the supervision of others, is not part of the formal training. Indeed, in many industries there is no way to replicate the job outside of the actual working environment. A new server in a restaurant would observe an experienced server and then attempt to perform the task on-the-job, usually under supervision. Indeed, in many industries there is no way to replicate the job outside of the actual working environment.

Advantages of on-the-job training	Disadvantages of on-the-job training
It allows workers to get early experience of the job at hand so that they can quickly tell if the job suits them.	Teaching and training is a specialist skill in itself and though an employee may be proficient themselves, that is no guarantee they will be able to teach others.
It is a cheaper way for businesses to train workers as there is no need for expensive trainers or workshop leaders and they are not paying the new employee to be absent from the workplace.	A trainer's own productivity will decline during the time taken to train others.
Employees will often enjoy on-the-job training as they may feel comfortable being supervised and coached by someone they know already in a less formal way than if an outsider were to do it.	In some cases, the trainer may pass on bad habits or encourage the trainee to cut corners.
This enables workers to access the required skills more quickly, and to become more productive within a shorter timeframe.	

Whilst at work employees may undertake **self-learning** by for example teaching themselves how to use a new piece of software. As technology is always changing and businesses adapt their practices and approaches training tends to be ongoing for most employees. Larger organisations tend to review their employees performance at work every year and during these reviews, **targets** are set for the following year. Training may be required for employees to meet these targets. Employees will record their progress and assess whether their targets have been met.

Performance reviews are usually formal and are carried out by an employee's line manager. 360 degree appraisals occur when evidence about a person's performance at work is gathered from a wide range of people from all aspects of their working life including colleagues and clients. A 360 degree appraisal of a CEO will include gathering data from: customers, directors, managers and workers at the bottom of the organisation's hierarchy.

The link between training, motivation and retention

Training can attract, empower and motivate workers as giving them training makes them feel as though they are valued by their employer. This can boost morale and, in turn, increase loyalty and **reduce staff turnover** – a large expense for businesses – and improve **staff retention**. In addition, a better trained workforce may not require as much supervision, which can lead to reduced staffing costs and allow businesses to explore more streamlined management structures.

Training **provides staff with new skills and knowledge** and improving the quality of the human resources should, in theory, make businesses more productive. It can also increase quality over and above that of rival firms to provide a competitive edge in the market. The business environment is a fast-moving one and forward-thinking firms will equip their employees with the skills and knowledge needed to better serve the customer, collaborate with each other more effectively, perform multiple job tasks (multi-skilling), use more sophisticated technology and understand new ways of working.

Why businesses train and develop employees: retraining to use new technology

Businesses need to **adapt to using new technologies and management practices** such as 3D printing (see Chapter 1.5.2) and just-in-time production (see Chapter 2.3.1). Businesses that failed to recognise these trends and the training needs associated with them would have risked being left behind and overtaken by their competitors. The introduction of new software, hardware and other types of technology will necessitate **retraining of employees**.

The Human Resources department is usually responsible for coordinating the training of staff. Businesses have many different types of training needs and the way that these are carried out varies according to the type of business in question.

Induction training for new staff

When a new member of staff is appointed it is an essential part of the settling in process that the employee is inducted into the company. This **induction training** varies from business to business but will often include:

- Orientation (taking a tour of the workplace).
- Introductions to key colleagues.
- An explanation of the organisational structure.
- Health and safety training.

Induction training should be geared towards helping to familiarise the employee with the job role and the business so that they become a productive member of the organisation more quickly. It is also common to teach the new staff member about the history, organisational culture and core values of the business, and to inform them about the standards and type of conduct expected.

Exam style question 1

Carlos Messi is a restaurateur from Buenos Aires, Argentina. He owns a chain of steak eateries. Training for staff in his kitchens is mostly done on-the-job. Carlos has recently recruited staff for a new outlet and is devising a training programme for them.

(a) State two things that might be included in the induction training for the new staff. *(2 marks)*

(b) Explain one benefit of conducting the training of the new staff on-the-job. *(3 marks)*

(c) Analyse whether Carlos should consider using off-the-job training for all kitchen staff in future. *(6 marks)*

Chapter review questions

1. Identify 3 different types of informal training.
2. Explain 3 advantages of on-the-job training.
3. Where might off-the-job training take place?
4. Explain 3 disadvantages of on-the-job training.
5. Why should businesses employ professional trainers to deliver training sessions?
6. Explain how training may be linked to performance reviews and target setting.
7. Why might an employee undertake self-learning?
8. How can training increase motivation?
9. Explain how training may improve staff retention.
10. Why is retraining needed to use new technology?

Key terms

360 degree appraisals occur when evidence about a person's performance at work is gathered from a wide range of people from all aspects of their working life including colleagues and clients.

Apprenticeships occur when a business employs somebody that does not have all of the skills required for the job and trains them for a period of time until they are skilled in a particular field.

Formal training is when an employee goes on a training course to learn a particular skill or acquire knowledge.

Induction training is training given to new employees to help them familiarise themselves with their new employer, role and working environment.

Informal training is where employees are trained whilst doing the job (**on-the-job training)** and this type of training does not lead to formal qualifications.

Off-the-job training is training whereby the business takes the employee away from the job in order to focus on learning the skills required in the role.

On-the-job training is training that is given to employees, usually by more experienced colleagues, whilst they are doing their job.

Performance reviews are usually an annual and formal review of an employee's performance at work usually carried out by an employee's line manager.

Retention of staff is the ability of a business to keep staff as they are happy and motivated workers.

Retraining is necessary to upskill employees through, for example, training them to use an updated type of software or a new piece of equipment.

Self-learning occurs when an employee, for example, teaches themselves how to use a new piece of software.

Training is the process of teaching employees to carry out their duties more effectively.

Chapter 2.5.4

Motivation

Aims

By the end of this chapter, students should be able to understand:

- the importance of motivation in the workplace.
- how businesses motivate employees: financial methods of motivation.
- how businesses motivate employees: non-financial methods of motivation.

The importance of motivation in the workplace

Motivation in the workplace is the willingness and desire to work hard and produce quality output. High levels of motivation amongst employees in a particular business will be **attractive to new employees** as it becomes commonly known that it is a good place to work and people want to work there. If employees are motivated the business will **retain staff** and **staff turnover** (the number of staff who leave in a year compared to the total number of staff) may be lower which will ensure a consistent performance and reduce recruitment costs.

Getting more out of your employees in terms of the quality and quantity of their work is a well-established strategy for businesses to increase profit. It might be that the **quality** (see Chapter 2.3.3) of the product can be improved because staff take more pride in their work, or it might be that production costs are reduced due to gains in output on the assembly line. **Absenteeism** (where workers are repeatedly absent from work), a key cost burden for business, will not be such a problem in a well-motivated workforce.

Motivation is the process of extracting better performance from the people in your business and therefore is related to levels of **productivity**.

Productivity refers to how efficiently factors of production are used to generate output. It is calculated by comparing the output to the factor input (see Chapter 2.3.1):

$$\textbf{Productivity} = \frac{\textbf{Output}}{\textbf{Input}}$$

The methods that a business chooses to increase motivation will be determined by the type of corporate culture the business has, the nature of the work done and the attitudes to leadership of the managerial personnel within the firm.

Financial methods of motivation

- **Remuneration** is the amount of money paid to an employee in return for their labour. It can take the form of monetary payment such as wages and salaries, and non-monetary rewards such as a company car, health insurance, old age pension and corporate membership of a sports club. Remuneration can be motivational but often the impact of a pay rise or increased benefits wears off quickly and employees soon perceive their new pay level as normal. Workers in this instance may also require non-financial methods to motivate them.

Types of remuneration – wages and salaries

Wages can be paid weekly or hourly. An hourly rate of pay is when a worker is paid a fixed amount for every hour they work. A salary is when workers are paid monthly.

- A **piece rate** is where an employee is paid a fixed amount for each unit of output produced. This can motivate them to produce as much as possible in a given time period in order to earn more money.

- A **bonus** refers to extra payments a worker can earn if they achieve pre-determined targets or perform well over a period of time (usually annually). The prospect of a high annual bonus may motivate workers to meet or exceed targets. However, a bonus earned which is lower than expected may be demotivational to an employee. Bankers are an example of an occupation that are often given very high annual bonuses as a motivational and retention tool. Workers who receive bonuses are often asked by employers to not reveal the amount of their bonus to others to prevent any potential demotivational effects.
- **Commission** is when employees are paid a percentage of the sales revenue that they generate for the company in addition to a basic salary. This method of payment is common in sales jobs such as selling property and insurance policies. Workers who earn commission are often paid a low basic salary and need to work hard to earn a reasonable salary. It can be stressful trying to meet targets; some workers, however, will earn very high levels of commission and this may be motivational to them.
- **Promotion** occurs when a worker moves up the organisation's hierarchy (see Chapter 2.5.1). This usually involves gaining more responsibility and status in the business as well as greater monetary rewards and is therefore likely to be motivational to an employee. However, if a person goes for a promotion and is overlooked then they may become demotivated.
- **Fringe benefits** are rewards an employee receives in addition to their salary which have a monetary value. These could be, for example, a company car or private health insurance. Employees may be motivated by receiving such perks but, as with remuneration, the novelty of receiving the perks may diminish with time and no longer prove to be motivational.
- **Profit sharing** is where firms may introduce a scheme whereby the employees are eligible to receive a share of the profits. This can motivate them to play their part in delivering increasing profits for the company.
- **Share ownership schemes** are where businesses offer shares to staff at preferential rates. If a worker is also a shareholder then they are given an incentive to work hard to contribute to increasing the profitability of the company.

Non-financial methods of motivation

Many businesses use non-financial in addition to financial methods to motivate employees which include: job rotation, job enrichment and autonomy.

- **Job rotation** occurs when a worker carries out a number of different roles in a business over a period of time. For example, a worker in a hotel may work on the reception desk, followed by work in the restaurant, bar and health centre. Providing workers with different roles within an organisation develops a range of skills and provides variety in the workplace; both of which may be motivational. Job rotation may allow an employee to discover their strengths and this may be motivational. Some workers may feel, however, demotivated when asked to perform particular tasks they do not like to do.
- **Job enrichment** can make a job more rewarding and interesting by allowing the worker to take on more responsibilities within their current role. For example, this might involve training catering staff in a large organisation to handle budgets and inventory. Workers develop new skills and have variety in their role which may be motivational. They may also receive training. It may however make a person's workload larger, which could lead to lower levels of motivation.
- **Job enlargement** can make a job more interesting and varied through expanding the range of tasks carried out within the role so that it becomes less specialised. For example, allowing a receptionist in a large firm to also manage a customer database. Employees acquire new skills and take on additional responsibility which may lead to higher levels of motivation. On the other hand, some workers may feel that their workload has increased without greater financial reward.
- Having **autonomy** at work allows employees to make decisions without asking permission from their superiors and to have greater control over what they do. Giving workers greater **autonomy** over their work can be motivational as it demonstrates a level of trust between employer and employee and it can

Team working can foster great camaraderie amongst staff, the pooling of skills and the sharing of ideas.

be empowering because employees can make decisions and carry out tasks independently. For example, if an architect is asked to take overall charge of a design project they may be excited and driven to produce excellent work. However, another person in the same situation may feel burdened by the extra tasks and this may lead to feelings of demotivation.

- Some large businesses, such as Google, encourage their workers to spend 20% of their time working on a project of their choice. It is sometimes called 'Genius Hour' and it encourages workers to pursue their own interests. Any original ideas they create belong to the business as they are devised on company time. This can greatly benefit the business and can be motivational for the worker.
- **Quality circles** are when workers are encouraged to meet regularly to discuss problems and find solutions to them. Workers tend to have firsthand knowledge of what works and what doesn't so managers should value their feedback. However, if managers ignore the suggestions of the quality circle, then it is likely these will not motivate.
- **Team working** can foster great camaraderie amongst staff, the pooling of skills and the sharing of ideas. The introduction of working practices can therefore spur productivity and motivation. However, teams can fail if there is not the right balance of skills and experience or individuals may encourage each other to shirk (avoid work).

Problems with non-financial motivation

- **Appropriateness** is a factor because some jobs are very difficult to enlarge or enrich. For example, security guards are there to watch over a building so it would not be appropriate for them to be given other tasks which might need all their attention and concentration, even for short periods.
- **Time, effort and cost** might be significant in setting up some of these schemes. For example, job enrichment may require large training budgets whilst quality circles necessitate time spent away from doing one's actual job. In the short run, this can be a big obstacle for many businesses. In addition, although job enrichment means the company may save on labour costs in the long run, it is important to note that such savings may take a long time to be realised.
- **Organisational inertia** can be a problem because change can be difficult to drive through in many organisations. New ways of working might therefore be difficult to implement, regardless of how well

the rationale for the change is explained. Furthermore, when job roles are changed there is often a suspicion that managers are increasing workloads but not increasing pay. This may actually harm rather than promote motivation within the business at the junior level, particularly if job losses are part of the reforms.

Exam style question 1

Chang's is a picture framing company based in the UK. Chang's purchases its products from a manufacturer based in Malaysia and has branches of the framing shops located throughout the country. It has traditionally relied on hourly rates of pay for its sales assistants and has never tried to implement any non-financial methods of motivation. The CEO of Chang's pays managers of each store a basic salary and a bonus based on the amount of goods sold.

(a) Explain how paying an hourly rate of pay to sales assistants will impact motivation in Chang's? *(3 marks)*

(b) Analyse the impact of a basic salary and bonus scheme on motivation levels of store managers. *(6 marks)*

Chapter review questions

1. What is meant by the term 'motivation'?
2. Explain the term productivity.
3. What are 'commission payments'?
4. Which type of job may attract a bonus?
5. Describe what is meant by job rotation and job enrichment.
6. Explain why having autonomy at work can be motivational.

Key terms

Absenteeism refers to employees that are frequently absent from work e.g. due to sickness.

Financial motivators refer to monetary incentives used to reward human effort, e.g. bonuses and commission payments.

Fringe benefits are rewards a person may get in return for their labour which have a monetary value such as health insurance.

Job enlargement is where an employer expands the range of tasks carried out within a job role so that it becomes less specialised.

Job enrichment is when a business makes a job more rewarding and interesting by allowing the worker to take more control over what they do.

Job rotation occurs when a worker carries out a number of different roles in a business over a period of time.

Motivation refers to the willingness of employees to give of their best effort in the workplace.

Non-financial motivators are factors other than increased pay which will encourage employees to increase their effort, such as team-working and job enrichment.

Remuneration is the amount of money paid to an employee in return for their labour.

Index